# Care & Advocacy

*Narratives from a School
for Immigrant Youth*

A volume in
*Educational Leadership for Social Justice*
Jeffrey S. Brooks, Denise E. Armstrong, Ira Bogotch, Sandra Harris,
Whitney Sherman, and George Theoharis, *Series Editors*

# Care & Advocacy

## Narratives from a School
## for Immigrant Youth

**Jo Bennett**

*Zayed University*

INFORMATION AGE PUBLISHING, INC.
Charlotte, NC • www.infoagepub.com

KH

**Library of Congress Cataloging-in-Publication Data**

Bennett, Jo.
  Care & advocacy narratives from a school for immigrant youth / Jo
Bennett.
      p. cm. – (Educational leadership for social justice)
  Includes bibliographical references.
  ISBN 978-1-61735-659-9 (pbk.) – ISBN 978-1-61735-660-5 (hardcover) –
ISBN 978-1-61735-661-2 (ebook)
  1. Children of immigrants–Education–United States–Case studies. 2.
Minority teenagers–Education–United States–Case studies. I. Title. II.
Title: Care and advocacy narratives from a school for immigrant youth.

  LC3746.B46 2011
  371.829–dc23
                                                          2011039437

Printed in the United States of America

6/28/13

# *Contents*

# Acknowledgements

This represents a rendering of my dissertation into a readable format. I wish to first express appreciation to my dissertation committee and professors at the University of Texas at Austin. Especially, I want to thank Pedro Reyes, for saying yes. Jay Scribner, who gave a wide-berth and vision for my ideas to grow. Terry Clark, for his imagination and help with organization. Emilo Zamora, for suggesting to ask about the participants' backgrounds and for his thorough reading. Cole Holmes, for caring. Julian Heilig Vasquez, for his respect. Angela Valenzuela, for knowing that students want to feel cared about. Doug Foley, who modeled using the narrative style for a study.

I wish to thank the teachers from my high school. I especially want to thank Mr. Forester, a nuclear physicist who decided teaching was his true vocation and Mr. Debill, who saw I needed special help and advocated for me. Also, Señora Thelma Lamb Ortiz de Montellaño for believing that she was Mayan in a past life.

I also want to thank my peers from high school, for they can be as important as the teachers.

I wish to thank my mentors at the Texas International Educational Consortium and at the University of Texas, especially Mary Kracklauer, John Schmidt, and Liz Murphy, for their support and contact over the past thirty years.

I wish to thank the teachers, parents, and students at Christa McAuliffe Elementary School, where I learned how to experience joy in educa-

---

*Care & Advocacy: Narratives from a School for Immigrant Youth*, pages ix–x
Copyright © 2012 by Information Age Publishing
All rights of reproduction in any form reserved.

tion while working as a parent with my children. I want to especially thank Angela Perino, Pat Steadman, Marile Shelly, Steve Trinwith, the founding teachers, and Mr. Clark, the first principal at the new school site. Also, I want to acknowledge the many students and families who became like family members at that school.

I wish to thank the administration, teachers, and staff at Newcomer Academy, where the study was conducted, especially Denise Norris, Ms. Terry, and Anabel Garza. I wish to thank the students who participated in the study and who attended the school.

I wish to thank my family and relatives, and all of those who came before, especially Aunt Dee Dee, who is like the Sibyl she is named after. Thanks to Pattye Henderson for her insights. Barbara Calaway, Maram Jadarat, Patrice Hein, Miranda Bennett, and Jill Wolf for support in preparation of the manuscript. And to Linda Bakken at Wichita State University for embracing me, as well as Jean Patterson for supporting this effort.

I wish to acknowledge Barbara McKinley and Ingleside Press for permission to use several poems throughout the manuscript. I want to thank Patrice Hein for the rendering of the path of the Monarch butterfly and the adaptation of the photo in Appendix E.

In closing, I would like to add that education is about more than academics; it's as much about human development.

# Series Editor's Preface

I am pleased to serve as series editor for this book series, *Educational Leadership for Social Justice*, with Information Age Publishing. The idea for this series grew out of the work of a committed group of leadership for scholars associated with the American Educational Research Association's (AERA) Leadership for Social Justice Special Interest Group (SIG). This group existed for many years before being officially affiliated with AERA, and has benefitted greatly from the ongoing leadership, support, and counsel of Dr. Catherine Marshall (University of North Carolina at Chapel Hill). It is also important to acknowledge the contributions of the SIG's first President, Dr. Ernestine Enomoto (University of Hawaii at Manoa), whose wisdom, stewardship, and guidance helped ease a transition into AERA's more formal organizational structures. This organizational change was at times difficult to reconcile with scholars who largely identify as non-traditional thinkers and push toward innovation rather than accepting the status quo. As the second Chair of the SIG, I appreciate all of Ernestine's hard work and friendship. I am now privileged to work under the leadership of Dr. Gaetane Jean-Marie, University of Oklahoma, the third chair of the LSJ SIG.

I am particularly indebted to my colleagues on the SIG's first Publications Committee, which I chaired from 2005–2007: Dr. Denise Armstrong, Brock University; Dr. Ira Bogotch, Florida Atlantic University; Dr. Sandra Harris, Lamar University; Dr. Whitney Sherman, Virginia Commonwealth University; and Dr. George Theoharis, Syracuse University. This committee was a joy to work with and I am pleased we have found many more ways to

*Care & Advocacy: Narratives from a School for Immigrant Youth*, pages xi–xii

collaborate as we seek to provide publication opportunities for scholarship in the area of leadership for social justice.

This book by Jo Bennett, the fourth in the series, breaks new ground in both content and presentation of research. In particular, the narrative style of the work makes her research accessible and powerful. We are exited to help provide a forum for this important voice in the ongoing conversation about equity and excellence in education, and the role(s) that leadership can assume in educational organizations.

Again, welcome to this fourth book in this Information Age Publishing series, *Educational Leadership for Social Justice*. You can learn more about the series at our web site: http://www.infoagepub.com/series/Educational-Leadership-for-Social-Justice. I invite you to contribute your own work on equity and influence to the series. We look forward to you joining the conversation.

—**Dr. Jeffrey S. Brooks**
Iowa State University

# *Preface and Dedication*

This is a book of oral narratives that have been collected from the participants of a school that was created for immigrant students. The stories from the students, teachers, administration, professional staff members, and support personnel document the importance of caring relationships in an educational setting.

These in-depth narratives were collected over time so as to capture a natural voice and reality from those whom we might not ordinarily hear in a school setting (Frisch, 1990; Gluck & Patai, 1991; Perks & Thomson, 1998). The narratives were gathered to show the benefits of these relationships as the participants themselves defined them. The interviews provide first-hand accounts of the experience of *caring* relationships and their impact on the school setting. Some questions that this framework raises include: Do students perform better academically when they feel cared for? Is caring for the students a strong enough glue for the students to remain in school and graduate? Will students, in turn, care for others? Will they behave morally in a school environment, and later, in their own community? If adults care for the needs of the students, will the students have the strength to persevere in difficult situations? If students feel that they have someone looking after them, do they develop character traits that will help them succeed in life? Is it enough if adults at home offer this caring support, or do teachers also need to show support?

The narratives have been analyzed for commonalities and differences (Mace, 1998) and adapted for the written page by deleting the unnecessary repetitions and hesitations found in normal speech patterns (Frisch, 1990).

In this book, the interview questions remain visible within the context of the questions and answers (Frisch, 1990; Perks & Thomson, 1998). By sharing large portions of the narratives, the hope is that the reader will feel the full context and power of the participants' words. Too often, the students' voices, or even those of staff members or teachers, are not heard in a school setting. In these narratives, we hear their voices directly. These narrations allow universal truths to emerge from the fullness of their interactions.

The narratives hearken from an oral literary heritage and blend well with the care theory and its focus on the relational aspects of teaching and learning. Oral narratives are often passed from one generation to another, and this tradition fosters relationships between family elders and the next generation. The narratives between the school elders and their students serve as a way of depicting the importance of the role adults play in the school setting. The blending of these three traditions—oral narratives, care theory, and intergenerational investigation—creates a merging of method and message that allows a rich and full account of the participants' experiences.

The profiles could come from any school. The teachers' backgrounds made the staff well suited for working with adolescent immigrants. The participants are from a two-year transitional, urban public high school for recent immigrants to the United States, situated in the south central part of the United States. The school is a pull-out program for adolescent immigrant students who place below third grade on a reading test. The contested issues surrounding how language is taught, whether pull-out or push-in programs are better, or other contested areas of teaching adolescent English learners in an urban setting are not the topic of this narrative.

I selected and described this school because it was a place where the teachers, students, and staff worked to support the students. This school emanated a feeling. As one of the founding teachers, I realized that stories could be told in the way the participants at this campus respected and honored each other and made the experience of school something special. The issues the students faced were as much about adolescence, loss of homeland, discrimination, and learning institutional processes in a new country and school system as they were about language learning.

I had contact with many students, teachers, administrators, and staff members over the four years of the study. I knew some students from teaching at the Newcomer Academy. Enrollment in my reading classes the first year reached 140 students. During the third year, which was the junior year for most of the students, I taught at Stafford High School, the neighborhood school that was the home school for a number of the Newcomer Academy students. Many of the students I knew transferred to Stafford.

I will never forget what it was like to run into them at Stafford. I was supposed to do my research at the Newcomer Academy while teaching at the neighborhood school down the hall, housed in the same building. Unfortunately I wasn't assigned to teach at that school. I was assigned to Stafford High School, across town. If I taught across town, I wasn't sure how I'd get my research done. Contemplating this difficulty, I put a wooden desk in my truck to bring to the new school. I was told, "You're an inclusion teacher. You won't have a desk here." That lack of consideration for how an already disappointed teacher would feel after hearing such news was a premonition of my experience at Stafford. Feeling a little dejected and wondering how I'd finish my study as planned, I began running into the Newcomer Academy students who had transitioned back to Stafford for their junior year on the first day of school—one or two here, another one there. Teddy. Veronica. Connie and her cousin, Vicky. It was like running into family members in this large, unwelcoming school. One day, while running an errand, I went to the computer lab and found five of the former Newcomer Academy students. They didn't have a permanent advisory teacher, and I didn't have an advisory.

I became their advisory teacher during their junior year, and my classroom became a home base for many of them until they got in trouble for skipping their own advisories. I also taught other Newcomer students who chose to remain at Stafford in lieu of attending the Newcomer Academy. Meeting them at the neighborhood school became an *"aha!"* moment for me. I realized that the students represented the school or its products, and that these graduates with whom I had developed relationships were the ones I needed to talk with—and study. Seeing how they survived and navigated the system after graduating from the Newcomer Academy was as important as describing their experience while there.

My contact with them during the fourth year of their high school experience was as a researcher, and I only saw the students occasionally for specific interviews or needs of the research. My contact with the students, administrators, teachers, and staff at the school over those four years has informed this study in varying capacities. Since their graduation, as I've run into those who participated in the study, they've kept me updated with details about their lives. My concerns and reflections about doing the research with these vulnerable populations are recorded in Appendix A, The Researcher's Stance.

## Use of Names

The name of the school and many of the participants are changed so that they can be anonymous. However, when I went to ask participants to look over the transcripts of their interviews, they told me they wanted to be named. At first I thought I would just mention them in the acknowledgements. With time, I decided to name the key informants and blend their names with the others, who will remain anonymous. The students are, of course, unnamed.

This book is dedicated to the first graduating class of students who attended the Newcomer Academy in its founding year. ¡No te olvides de Mexico! Don't forget Mexico or the other home countries that you gave up when you traveled to the United States to make it your new home!

—**Jo Bennett**
Wichita, Kansas and Austin, Texas

# Background and Rationale of This Study

Throughout most of the 20th century, schools educated well about one third of their young charges. Another 40 percent were schooled but hardly well educated. And about a quarter of the children were left behind all together. (Murphy et al., 2001; Powell, Farrar, & Cohen, 1985; Sedlack, Wheeler, Pullin, & Cusick, 1986)

Poor minority children were disproportionately clustered in these latter two groups. The great tragedy here is that the profession's 100-year infatuation with management practices and chunks of knowledge from the behavioral sciences rarely pushed the field of school administration to acknowledge, let alone address, this reality.

The Interstate School Leaders Licensure Consortium (ISLLC) found this unacceptable. In reaching that conclusion, we developed a platform that demands, as one critic of the Standards laments, *"school leaders (who) wield political and legal levers to advance social justice."* (Hess, 2003, p. 14) (Murphy, 2005)

This study is located at the intersection of social justice, educational leadership, and the care ethic. That is, the story begins where the interactions between adults and students take place in a process called learning. It documents the value of positive interactions and exchanges in the development of relationships between teachers and their students (Noddings, 1984, 2003; Valenzuela, 1999) as a significant but often-overlooked aspect of the urban school setting. The high turnover rate of teachers (Darling-Hammond, 2003; Wilson, Floden & Ferrini-Mundy, 2001) and the high dropout rate of urban high school students (Orfield, 2004; Romo & Falbo, 1996;

Swanson, 2006, 2008; Texas Education Agency [TEA], 2001, 2009; Valenzuela, Fuller, & Vasquez-Heilig, 2006; Vasquez-Heilig, 2011) point to the lack of this relationship development. These two phenomena are often not discussed in relation to each other. The importance of positive experiences for both the teachers and students has not been adequately documented in the accountability conversation nor has it been given a place in pre-service, in-service, or professional development discussions for school leadership or teacher preparation.

The teacher preparation conversation has often not focused on this taken-for-granted aspect of the educational dynamic. If you ask teachers, invariably they will respond that they went into teaching because of the students. It is why many of us went into teaching, yet we work in systems that do not always allow that to happen, especially if we have to be more concerned about policies than about caring for students as individuals. Indeed, after performance, learning about content, classroom management, and socio-economic awareness, coaching in any other area is almost non-existent. Additionally, in leadership preparation programs, the importance of social and emotional aspects of working with staff and, in turn, the staff with their students is not given space. How to encourage positive interpersonal skills, create positive relationships and to allow them to flourish is also either taken for granted or given little space in leadership development programs. Leadership preparation usually consists of six strands or standards—the ISLLC standards, which include the following strands: creating a shared vision; sustaining a culture of inclusiveness and learning by all, including the faculty; promoting a safe and effective learning environment; embracing community and parents; acting with fairness and equity; and influencing and understanding the political, socio-economic and cultural context (Council of Chief State School Officers, 1996).

An acknowledgement of the importance of the affective domain, such as social emotional learning and character development, is now included in some course syllabi across the United States but is not given a central role in leadership preparation programs or included in the leadership dispositions or knowledge base of the ISLLC standards. A focus on management more than on students, learning, and teaching in the past (Donaldson, 2001) spurred the development of the new standards. The added emphasis on creating community in schools is discussed in creating professional learning communities. A missing piece seems to be on how to bring about these changes. Collaboration is encouraged (Hargreaves, 2008a, 2008b; Leithwood & Mascall, 2008; Miller & Rowan, 2006; Spillane, 2006; Spillane & Diamond, 2007), but without guidance on how to create and develop interpersonal and intrapersonal skills.

## Professional Learning Communities

In theory, a learning community involves students, teachers, and administrators engaged in learning together (Knight, 2007; Hord, 2004). The professional learning community continuously seeks to share learning and act on this shared knowledge with a goal of enhancing the effectiveness of all the adults involved in the learning organization for the students' benefit. Often the teachers are organized to work in teams, so that information can easily be shared and distributed among the group for the sake of the students. A healthy team situation would involve dialogue and a sense of reciprocity, as exemplified in the way teachers create reciprocal relationships between themselves and the students. Ideally, the goals are created and set by the teams themselves, thereby allowing the teachers to feel empowered. When the teachers feel empowered, they more readily share that sense with the students.

## Multicultural Professional Learning Communities

One aspect of shared information in a professional learning community team would be knowledge about the students' backgrounds as well as their academic issues. An awareness of the socio-cultural context of the community can help teachers, staff, and administrators understand the issues in which the school is surrounded and embedded. Working to understand the issues of the community and understanding students and their families as individuals can help school practitioners create a sense of social justice by addressing the overall development of the students. This awareness to work with a student as a whole child, while encouraged in the development of learning communities (Nieto, 1999) and in the literature (Hord, 2004; Knight, 2007), does not always come to the fore in schools (Stanton Salazar, 1997; Valencia, 1997; Valenzuela, 1999).

Social justice is a complex and multi-faceted concept or process. It has been suggested that we can understand social justice by how it shows in our actions regarding academic achievement, in a critical consciousness, and by putting inclusive practices in place (Grant & Sleeter, 2007; Theoharis, 2009). Furman and Gruenewald (2004) suggest that the present accountability policy environment of education detracts from the important purposes of education, such as developing a community and other important *"moral purposes"* (p. 48, emphasis added). Bogotch (2002) suggests that social justice is a deliberate intervention that requires the moral use of power by school leadership. Questions in general about how power is used by administration, teachers, and other adults in a school setting with regard to the students or learners is at the heart of the care literature (Beck, 1994; Beck & Murphy, 1994; Doehring, 1995; Marshall, 1992; Marshall & Anderson, 1995; Noblit, 1993; Rusch & Marshall, 1995; Sergiovanni & Starratt, 2002; Sernak, 1998).

## Social Justice and the Care Ethic

The idea of a moral obligation in education is taken for granted as the purpose behind learning, but it is somehow tucked aside when there is a need for accountability, classroom control, or other issues where the individual experience or right is placed beneath the needs of a broader good for the community. Often, views that put students' experiences first are seen as alternative visions and, as such, are often not rewarded or even put forth (Marshall & Gerstl-Pepin, 2005).

In this study, social justice is defined as beginning with the interaction of one to another; that is, with the way in which participants in a community or culture interact with each other. This interaction has deep implications for administrators,' teachers,' and students' sense of empowerment, improvement in performance, and the ability to imagine a vibrant future. Indeed, protecting the space for transformative experiences to take place in schools can be inextricably linked to school leadership (Senge, Cambron-McCabe, Lucas, Smith, Dutton, & Kleiner, 2000). Yet, these understandings are swept aside for the sake of testing and hold teachers and students accountable to test scores rather than an accountability to moral development, social justice, or a sense of holding to the greater good. Likewise, adjustments that must be made for interacting with students from different socio-cultural backgrounds or with language learning issues are not always areas that are understood.

## Adolescent Immigrant Learning Issues

Indeed, the study of adolescent immigrant students encompasses many contested issues and is a complicated terrain. Some of the issues include those of socio-economic context, language learning, cultural adjustments, high dropout and low graduation rates, as well as school environments that may themselves be unstable and unwelcoming. While there are probably schools that successfully address many of these issues, the focus of this study began with the importance of relationships. It is hard to find a school that addresses all of the complex issues successfully. Once teachers initiate relationships with students and are given the support and space by the administration to do so, the day-to-day issues facing students begin to surface.

The language learning issues and cultural adjustments are two of the most pressing needs that surface inside the school environment while family obligations and economic pressures can be external contributing factors that can interfere with positive school environments.

## Language Issues

The controversies surrounding how English language learners (ELL) students should best be educated are age old and sometimes fractious (Chamot & O'Malley, 1994; Echevarria, Short, & Vogt, 2007; Gibbons & Cummins, 2002; Krashen, 2010; Scarcella, 2003a, 2003b). Conversations about how to teach language, in general, are often fraught with intense debates over a one best method. Is a phonics-based approach or whole language approach, embracing the love of literature, a better approach? The same debate plays out with second language learning, where some feel that a natural approach and exposure to the language is enough for a student to learn, while others espouse that a strong grammar and structural base are necessary to build proficiency. Debates about whether students should be pulled out or pulled in; taught grammar or allowed to pick up language though natural usage; pushed with English only classes or allowed a bilingual, dual language approach are only some of the questions that continue and are ongoing. Perhaps one reason this is such a contested area is that identity is often expressed through language, and our approach to language is therefore as multifaceted as our individualism.

In truth, an answer depends on a multitude of considerations. What is the age of the student? How much education has the student had before coming to the United States? What is the inclination of the student? What is the curriculum? What is the expertise of the teacher? What is the support throughout the campus? Because learning is an individual process, it is hard to accommodate all of the individual variations and needs if there is not an awareness of these alternatives and viable options offered and support mechanisms in place for a variety of delivery options. An added issue with adolescent immigrant students is that there is not a lot of time for mistakes, and there are not often enough resources to offer the number of choices needed. The students must begin studying content classes in the new language if they are to graduate in four years. While most agree that it takes from five to seven years for academic language development to take place, students can be put in situations where language production is modified, and in the first two to three years, limited proficiency is supported.

Because of the time constraints in high schools, some argue for a dual language program, with content classes offered in the native language. This idea could be accommodated in Spanish or another language, if there are large numbers of students speaking a second language. Again, limited resources and time constraints become a limiting factor in the choices. While solutions that serve a majority of students have been developed and accommodate the majority of the students, those who may need more structure to learn or who had an interrupted education may not be given the language resources they need: a lab, in-class support on projects or assignments and/ or an option to graduate in five years (without this being seen as punitive). Instead of changing the school day, often after-school individual tutoring is the band-aid solution offered to many students. The ability to modify education for each student is said to be a goal for all of those who work in public education, but the constraints of time, resources, personnel, and our isomorphic notions about what schools should look like can make this notion challenging.

Once students start to drop behind in classes, or see that they will not graduate with their peers, they often do a free fall and drop out, without a safety net to catch them.

## Border Crossing and Cultural Issues

Immigrant students, by definition, are students who have left their homes and often must learn not only a new language but also a new culture. Border crossing and the resultant growth and adaptations can be painful experiences in the way that any growth experience can be, even if it brings new and desired results. Think of what it is like to join a sports team. This is perhaps something you have always dreamed of, only to find out that exercising every day in the hot sun, being knocked down repeatedly by team mates, and the constancy of coaches' corrective directions is a lot harder than you imagined it would be. While it is rewarding, it is also a lot of work and takes focus, desire, and an internal compass that helps you get to the finished result.

Add to this growth experience though, an element that may not be present in the sports example. What if you didn't want to come? What if it was your parent's idea or something you had to do out of economic or political necessity? Many students come to the classroom with a need for something to make sense, and a strong relationship with an adult can create that highway to knowledge and sense-making that the head, heart, and gut so desperately crave. Students want to learn; learning is a natural part of being a human being. Learning in a new language, in a new country, with a culture that is often perceived as cold or unconcerned can sometimes add insult to injury or a sense of disconnectedness that students are not able to bear. This loss of connection with the school often compounds the profound sense of loss already felt from leaving their home.

## Student Dropout Rate

Language learning issues can be a reason some Latino students don't make the adjustment. Additionally, the care literature shows us that students do not feel cared for when their needs are not being met (Cushman, 2005; Noddings, 2003). Students who do not feel their needs are addressed at school drop out for any number of reasons, creating an issue of national importance. Recent studies suggest that the numbers supplied by school districts are staggeringly higher than previously thought. When cohort groups of students are studied—that is, when we look at a group of incoming freshmen through the four years of high school, rather than a snapshot of those who graduated—the numbers of students actually remaining in school and graduating are much smaller. The numbers can vary according to who collects the data and the techniques that have been used, but the fact remains that dropout rates are high—whether we assume the school graduation figures of 80 percent or higher or 30 to 50 percent, as cited in other studies (Swanson, 2008; TEA, 2001, 2009; Valenzuela, Fuller, & Vasquez-Heilig, 2006).

I have seen that students in urban schools drop out for any variety of personal reasons: issues with girlfriends or boyfriends; anger at teachers, for a particular event or in general because of a general sense of frustration; the need for financial support; or a lack of connection between the school and their lived reality, to name only a few reasons students let go of the opportunities a high school diploma can bring. If students felt a connection to the school and felt the importance of what their teachers were doing, many of the reasons for dropping out would not matter to the degree that they do.

At the end of the ninth grade many students fall behind because, as one told me, "Miss, they don't understand." It appears that students have learned how to navigate the system by building in their own supports. By failing and taking the class a second time, students are able to understand the concepts and pass the class. The ninth-grade populations at many schools across the nation have a ninth-grade swell because of the number who enter and then repeat these classes for a myriad of reasons, one of which is lack of language ability. If we follow the students to the senior year, we can see that fewer of these students actually graduate from the school or district. Mobility and transfer can account for some of this attrition, but anecdotal accounts and onsite research show that many students just stop coming for a number of personal and academic reasons. Unfortunately, students often have to fail to get what they want or need.

The relational aspect of the care theory suggests that the need to retain teachers and the need to decrease the student dropout rate is a related issue. Since the majority of the participants at a school are made up of teachers and students, their combined needs are the primary concern, the technical core, of any school. Students who are wrapped in the mantle of caring relationships are not so easily swayed by distractions or a sense of directionlessness, and can put personal issues and goals in perspective. Academic performance improves when personal issues are resolved. The fact that teachers and students are both leaving schools suggests that the benefit they can bring to each other is not being realized in schools. The high turnover of faculty affects the learning environment, school culture, and organizational operations. Simply put, how can schools and school systems expect students to remain in school and complete their studies successfully with such a high turnover in teachers?

Caring relationships are even more important when education takes place in a multi-cultural setting where family ties and a collective identity are important (Campbell, 2004; Nieto, 2003; Valenzuela, 1999). With the rapidly changing demographics (Lee & Bean, 2004; Louis, 2003; Reyes, Scribner, & Scribner, 1999), a new teacher will likely work in an urban area of mixed ethnicities, including Latino, African American and Vietnamese, as well as European American (Cochran-Smith, 1995; Ladson-Billings, 2009; Wright, Houston, Ellis, Holloway, & Hudson, 2003). If education is to be responsive to the changing sociological needs (Meyer & Rowan, 1991; Reyes et al., 1999; Valenzuela, 1999), then it is important we understand how teachers can form meaningful, caring relationships with students in their pursuit of knowledge and character development, across cultures.

## Teacher Dropout Rate

The preparation, retention, and support involving new teachers are matters of great discussion in literature today (Brown & Wynn, 2007; Darling-Hammond, 2000, 2003; Hanushek, Kain, & Rivkin, 1998, 1999, 2004; Ingersoll, 2001a, 2001b, 2002, 2003; Wilson, Floden, & Ferrini-Mundy, 2001). With the focus directed by the No Child Left Behind (NCLB) legislation, prominent teacher research and conversations for federally funded research cover teacher quality (Darling-Hammond, 2004), teaching within the core area of preparation (Ingersoll, 1998), and new teacher supports (Ingersoll, 2001a, 2001b; Darling-Hammond, 2003).

Although pay and other factors influence the teacher attrition rate, Ingersoll (2001a) found that teacher participation in decision making, administrative support, and school climate are all statistically associated with teacher turnover. Teachers need to connect with their students, but they need to know they have support from school leadership and that their decisions will influence the environment in which they function. A teacher's sense of empowerment can influence whether the teacher is able to participate in genuinely caring and supportive relationships with students. Kelly (2004) found that undesirable working conditions, specifically the behavioral climate of the schools, also increased the dropout rates of teachers. If students do not feel supported by teachers and teachers in turn do not feel supported by leadership, then a cyclical process of teachers and students dropping out begins and perpetuates itself. Stockard and Lehman (2004) found that new teachers reported lower rates of satisfaction with teaching when they felt they had less influence over their work, less support, less effective leadership, and when the schools in which they taught had higher rates of student behavioral problems. Schools vary widely with regards to how teachers feel about themselves, their work, and their students. The differences from one school to another show us how important leadership can be with regard to a school setting. Leadership can play an important role in offering support for new teachers.

## Role of Leadership in Teacher Retention

The building leader can develop and encourage a teacher's sense of autonomy and efficacy, and at the same time, create a space for collaboration, by as small a gesture as adjusting the schedule for team meetings. Additionally, more and more, teachers have to work together as they share data with one another and share information about students. That means that school leaders need to give building teams and teamwork a priority in school planning and schedules. Brown and Wynn (2007) have documented many sources in their reviews that show a positive teaching experience can not only support the retention of new teachers but also be a predictor of student performance (especially, they cite the Berry & King report for the Southeast Center for Teaching Quality, 2005).

Schools as learning centers, where veteran and new teachers are supported to interact freely, can create networks of relationships that support teachers when working with their students. The relationships they form are typically empowering rather than hierarchical in nature. Louis, Marks, and Kruse (1996) found that a collaborative practice, focused on student learning and coupled with reflective practices, supports double-loop learning, or a learning process that grows and adapts over time (Argyris, 1999; Senge et al., 2000). Additionally, Theoharis (2009) has noted that inclusiveness and courage are integral factors when implementing social equity and fairness in reaching all students in a learning community.

This study posits that the fundamental basis or starting point of social justice in schools today is the manner in which participants relate to one another. This includes how teachers interact and support students; how veteran teachers interact and support new teachers; and how school leadership creates the tone for these interactions to take place and, in general, help the teachers feel supported and respected with their needs for positive school-wide behavior and culture, curricular needs, and ongoing professional development.

Brown and Wynne (2007) suggest that new teachers need contextualized support while they are engaged in act of teaching. In citing Feiman-Nemser (2003), they note that new teachers will not always know their needs in advance; hence, the need for the ongoing interrelatedness with other staff members, peer support and on-going professional development. The highly interactive and spontaneous nature of teaching explains why relationship development among multiple stakeholders at various levels is so vital and important.

## Cultural Issues in Retention

Leadership development, especially as rearticulated by the ISLLC Consortium (Murphy, 2005) and as supported by the National Council for the Accreditation of Teacher Education (NCATE) adoption of double-loop learning standards, encourages continuous and transformational learning models among the preparation programs, school districts, and other community stakeholders (Cibulka, 2009). The formation of these partnerships points to the need for collaborative professional organizations and efforts in order to meet today's leadership challenges (for example, see Darling-Hammond, LaPointe, Meyerson, Orr, & Cohen, 2007). The importance and awareness of community and, by implication, parental involvement and community engagement has been added to the ISLLC standards and leadership development, and while important, it needs further commitment, development, and focus by all of the stakeholders (Murphy, 2005). The teacher and school leadership working to understand the cultural context of the students, their families, and the community the students live in could facilitate the development of a bridge across one of the biggest cultural divides. This border must be crossed if meaningful interactions are to take place on the highway created between the teacher and student.

At present, the responsibility to navigate between the world of the school and that of their parents rests on the shoulders of the youngsters. Expecting the students to be the ambassadors of that change process places an incredible burden on them. If teachers can create their classrooms in a way that enables them to listen to students, then the relationship building and the border-crossing process can begin to take place. Campano (2007) suggests that teachers can learn a great deal by listening to the quiet authority of children. When two cultures come together, one must concede and bow to the other (Hofstede, Hofstede, & Minkov, 2010). It would make sense that the adults in a school setting take on the role of stewardship in linking the worlds in which the students must live and negotiate. Further, by inviting the parents to be a part of the educational process, it is recognizing their role in the lives of the school children.

## Location of the Study

Many will agree that the technical core, or learning, is the most important aspect of schools and that this learning takes place in the classrooms. Learning can be characterized by the interaction among the teachers, curriculum, and students. Merit pay is now proposed for teachers whose students perform better on standardized tests (see, for example, the United States Department of Education website for the current conversation). The idea that teachers can cause improved performance is a testimony to the difference a good teacher can make. In the K–12 environment we know that this is not just because one teacher knows more than another (although this may be the case) or that one has better knowledge of how to break the information down for the student, it is also because the teacher knows how to turn the student toward learning. School change begins in the classroom, or more specifically, within this complex teacher student dynamic (Lampert, 2010). Teachers are the ones who create the rapport, caring, and empathy of which Goldman (2006) speaks in his discussion of the importance and reason for social intelligence. These emotions are the cornerstone of the practice and creation of caring experiences in schools.

A turning point at a school is often marked by a leader, who changes the tone to create equitable, meaningful, and sustained change toward social justice. An emphasis on positive experiences is as important as academic outcomes because it is in these initial stirrings or relationship development that students gain the confidence to create and connect with the knowledge the teacher is presenting, to take imaginative leaps and risks, and to move their notions of knowledge, life, and identity to something beyond their present worldviews. How we relate to one another is the starting point toward social justice. I heard recently on a public announcement for the Boys and Girls Club, " It only takes one caring adult to make a difference in a child's life." Cushman (2005) confirms this idea as well. A nationwide coalition says it takes a group of adults in a child's life to make a difference (see www.americaspromise.org). Whatever the number, the power of a caring adult inside or outside the classroom can be the springboard and navigator for a student to move to the next level.

The study is located, then, at the juncture where that relationship between a teacher and a student begins. This place is at once tenuous and strong. It exists in the minds, hearts, and psyches of the students as well as of the teachers. It is hard to say where it begins and ends. And it is hard to say who carries more of the responsibility for its development or how it begins. So while we often attribute learning to a place, it may begin at a school, but its exact location may not be known.

At first I thought the study would be located at one school site, the Newcomer Academy where adolescent immigrants with low language ability began their academic journey in the United States. But when it came time to conduct the study, the students I studied had already transitioned to their neighborhood schools as juniors and seniors. Unplanned encounters with my former students helped me understand that they needed to be the subjects of my study and were the participants I needed to interview. A third space that Bhabha (1994) speaks of, created through a complex manner of interaction and conceptualization, was the place or location where my students and I began to interact and relate with each other. This universal setting, this space between the culture of the student and the culture of the teacher is the basis of all schools, and as such, gave this study a certain universal appeal, beyond the experiences of immigrant students, who hail from another culture.

When there are barriers in building a bridge between the teacher and student, one or both works to remove the barriers, and in the case of special populations or collective issues, the teachers may need help beyond their previous experiences. The institution may need to create supports and facilitate the bonding so that the transformational experience that draws teachers to their profession and the resultant learning that motivates students to come back day in and day out can take place.

E. M. Forster, in his book *A Room with a View* (1988), uses the metaphor of a room without a view as one where the inhabitants look inward while the room with a view allows the inhabitants to look out at a new world beyond one that has been known before. The first group travels from one country to another as tourists, only knowing a new culture or country through the world of the five-star hotel. In the room with a view, a visitor to a new culture and daily life can see the world the citizens of that country know. In the same way, the location of this study is like that room with a view, where the relationship with a teacher can create a new and illuminating outward looking space, which allows for growth and transformation to take place, by knowing the other in a real way and not in a way colored by a generalized notion of what a student should do.

Many of us can remember a favorite teacher. We may remember an unexpected gesture or a surprise show of attention or understanding by a teacher that made us realize that this teacher was thinking of us or understood us. This care or this relational aspect of teaching is remembered long after what the teacher actually taught us has gone. This connection and understanding is what the immigrant student, away from her home, in a new, unknown culture, longs for.

I remember two or three teachers who touched me in a deep way because of their understanding of me as an individual or because of the depths they could take me to with the subject matter. This ability for the teacher to touch us is something we all crave, some more than others. Students who understand a subject, who come from a home with warm supports, or who have an inclination for a topic of study, may not need the individual guidance, attention, or gesture from the teacher. It is sometimes the weaker student who needs a helping hand, and especially needs to be touched in a deep or caring way. Teachers can help students create a liking for the educational process, give the student the background in order to grasp a topic, or help the student relax enough for education to begin. Students who travel at the edge of a classroom long to be touched in a deep way to allow their imaginations to take root in something solid.

Tobias Wolff (2004) speculates on the role of imagination in the transformation process of a students' psyche in a young child's life. When a student has to make an exceptionally high leap, the student's imagination in connecting to something concrete, through the teacher, makes the gap that must be spanned achievable, becoming a leap that is within reach. It is on this roadway of the relationship that the needed changes take place. The role of the imagination in the change process—both personally and for the school as a whole—is an element that is not often discussed in school changes. Imagination connected with a mentor or a caring adult can take a student beyond the wildest reaches of the mind. Left to its own devices, it can lead a youngster into unwanted areas and dark corners. The utilizing of emotions to grow with the help and support of peers and adults who genuinely care for each individual is one of the most powerful forces on this earth.

A teacher, who can see a discouraged student, can know the obstacles and roadblocks a student may experience from knowing the student and by knowing the subject and has the power to turn a youngster around by simply sitting down and saying, "Let's figure this out." Classrooms and schools have to be set up in such a way that the teacher or an adult can be available to students in this way.

As time went by, and the more I worked on the study, I began to realize that the school settings where these students continued their studies make a difference in the way that teachers can respond to students' needs. And even though the Newcomer Academy is where the study took place, in truth, this study took place in the relationships between me, as a former teacher and a researcher, and the students who transformed me as much as they may have been helped.

## Relationship as the Path to a Global Way of Knowing

The new immigrant students have crossed political and cultural borders and they need, as other students do, for teachers to meet them halfway on that journey, to help bridge that distance that must be traveled. Awareness of the loss or grief and the resultant emotions that surface or remain just below the surface are becoming known more and more in intercultural conversations about a third space (Bhabha, 1994; Rimmington & Alagic, 2009; Rutherford, 1990; Van Reken & Pollock, 2009). In our modern, mobile world, this kind of understanding will become more common as people live in multiple cultures or countries and are children of mixed ethnicities, cultures, and worldviews. There is a sense of loss, but also a wider worldview, a sense that home is everywhere, and a longing to connect with others who understand this way of knowing. A longing for connection is what starts the bridge with the teacher. As more teachers become mobile and world travelers themselves, they will naturally develop broader worldviews, and the easier it will be for them to relate to and connect with students from other cultures. The teachers will actually crave that experience as much as the students do, as they will understand what it is like to move between two or three cultures and hold this new multiple identity as their native identity. Moving from loss to gain and from one country to another, the students travel with the teacher on *El Camino Real*.

*In the end it wasn't*
*technically so challenging*
*or difficult,*
*as a matter of will power.*
*And on returning,*
*keeping the summit ever ahead.*
*. . . keeping the silence within*
*while moving midst*
*color and sound.*

—Barbara McKinley, *Second Verse* (2006, p. 12)

# 1

# *The Newcomer Academy*

*All the world's a stage . . . and all the men*
*and women, merely players.*
—William Shakespeare (*As You Like It*)

## Introduction

This book describes relationships that formed in an urban school created specifically for recent immigrants. This institutional setting, where the teaching and learning took place, framed the interactions among the adults and their students. As Scott (2001) described, the institutional constraints are regulatory, normative, and cultural in nature. The memory-laden paths of institutions that make up public schools change very slowly and form in predictable ways (Powell & DiMaggio, 1991). This chapter shows that although the routine of a school can be predictable, noticeable differences can surround the experience of school and schooling itself for the students. The overall school culture and strength of the interactions within it can pull students toward the school or push them away toward peers or forces outside of the school.

*Care & Advocacy: Narratives from a School for Immigrant Youth,* pages 1–12
Copyright © 2012 by Information Age Publishing
All rights of reproduction in any form reserved.

This book has been written on the premise that a school and its cultural context can make a difference in a student's life and education. In her award-winning book, *The Good High School,* Lawrence-Lightfoot documented a process for researching schools. She spoke of the need for readers to place studies in a context, "to visualize the terrain, the community, the neighborhood streets, and the people" (Lawrence-Lightfoot, 1983, p. 22). The notion of illustrating a context for a study of a high school, and thus creating a more thorough representation, came from Lawrence-Lightfoot's experiences with portraits and portraiture.

With this point in mind, I describe the stage or location in which the students, teachers, and administrators who shared their stories in this book played out their parts. The Newcomer Academy, a two-year program for recent immigrant high school students, is the focal point of the conversation: The students all spent their first two years at this school, after which they transitioned to their neighborhood home schools for their junior and senior years. The book describes two of the neighborhood high schools. One was next door to the Newcomer Academy, and many of the students chose to enroll at this school in order to use the Academy as a continued support in their lives. The other school was a neighborhood high school from which most of the students transitioned and later returned to finish their junior and senior years. The three schools tell different stories and create different effects and impressions on the students; for this reason, all three schools are described. One could argue that a school structure or edifice does not form the boundaries for the relationships between students and their teachers. However, I found that this was not the case from my own experiences, which will be woven throughout the context of this narrative. The institutional framework does make a difference in the way a teacher can react to her students and how the students are served and experience their education.

The names of the schools have been fictionalized but otherwise remain true to their original identities. The book describes the physical features of the school sites and gives an overview of the student population. It depicts the hallways of the schools, where we often see students being themselves, and it mentions cultural aspects of the school. Further, it details the schools' restructuring vision, articulates the curriculum and performance indicators, and shares other aspects of the school. It is hoped that these descriptions will give a sense of the school setting, where the students spend their time, and provide an idea of the school's influence on their shared and collective attitude toward school.

The students of the Newcomer Academy transition to the district neighborhood schools after their first two years at the academy.[1] We see a continuum of the students' journeys from their home countries to the Newcomer Academy as freshmen and sophomores, and then their transition to the neighborhood school close to their home.[2] Despite the extra attention given to them at the academy during their first two years, only a handful of the students graduated after the full four years upon their return to their neighborhood schools.[3]

## Why This School?

It is somewhat disheartening to know that after so much time, effort, and resource allocation for these students during their first two years of school, so few students actually graduated after transitioning to their neighborhood home school. I do not have a way of knowing how many actually graduated, as some may have moved to another community or back to Mexico. But from anecdotal information, I know that only one in five or six students graduated in four years. Some went on to work toward their GED, went into the military, or chose other options. Others who graduated worked in restaurants, attended local university or colleges, or started families.

The adults and students talked about the Newcomer Academy as a special place. When I asked students at their neighborhood home school which Newcomer Academy teacher I should interview, they would say, "Any of them, Miss." This school was the starting point for the teachers and students. In talking about the schools, it is not to suggest that all of the issues were resolved: How language should be taught, how students should be assessed, how students should be monitored after leaving the Newcomer Academy, how decisions were made, and even where the school should be located were all contested areas of conversation. The students took buses from their neighborhood school to the second school, JFK, and then rode one or two buses to Newcomer, making a daily two-hour bus journey. As a solution, some proponents thought that the capacity at the two neighborhood home schools could be built up to accommodate the students at the school where they would then stay. The Newcomer Academy would have two hubs—a north and a south campus—and the schools where the students transitioned would then be ready to receive them.

The focus of this study and the reason for describing the schools is to attempt to document what was working and how the adults in the school created a respectful, fun environment focused on learning. Students, after all, develop relationships with teachers and come to school to learn.

## Newcomer Academy

This book describes the school history, curriculum and performance indicators, restructuring vision and challenge, hall culture, physical appearance, and student and staff population demographics as a way to bring the school to life for the reader.

### School History

The Newcomer Academy is a newly created school established in 2004 for high school international students, or recent immigrants to the United States. If students scored at a third-grade reading level or lower on their English placement tests, they were invited to attend this school. Parents could choose to send their children to a neighborhood or home school, despite the fact that a home school may not have the resources to serve their children's needs. In the words of Anabel, the founding principal of the Newcomer Academy:

> It is a new school in the school district. It was established first as part of Robert E. Lee High School with every intention to make it its own campus. We became an independent high school in the second year. The purpose of this school is to serve new immigrant students who have never been to any school in the United States. The goal of the school is to transition students successfully from this two-year program into the mainstream high school, where they will be able to function in the mainstream classrooms.

Just like the principal, I was hired a few days before the school opened. The first year, the six teachers walked the students to their buses and then met after school with the principal at least two days a week, or sometimes more, to sit around a table and discuss school matters. The principal gave the teaching staff a good deal of influence during the first semester. She allowed them to shuffle students to adjust their placement as language abilities became known, and to adjust as some students began to make progress after settling into a routine. A great deal of chaos, as well as flexibility, surrounded the weekly adjustments that took place.

Each subsequent year, the process became more systematic as patterns in language placement issues, curricular decisions, and staff training began to coalesce. Further, the counselor and assistant principal almost exclusively dealt with placements of students and schedules after the first year, which removed decisions from the first-hand knowledge the teachers had about the students. With time, demands and constraints from district-level management began to dominate the agendas of the teachers' meetings. During the second year, the teaching staff almost doubled, and the teachers began to work in teams at scheduled times during the school day. Although a good deal of discussion took place among the teams on Tuesdays, the meetings with the principal on Thursdays were often for the purpose of staff development. They could be characterized as *talking memos*, in which the principal informed and the teachers listened.

After the first year, the teachers no longer met after school but rather with their teams on Tuesdays and Thursdays during a common planning time in what were called *horizontal teams*. The teams consisted of six or seven teachers who shared the same 100–140 students and taught the various core content subjects: world history, algebra, reading, language arts, and biology. On Tuesdays, the teams discussed issues pertaining to students and common concerns among the teachers. On Thursdays, the teams met with the principal for staff development. Vertical teams, or discipline area teams, met after school or during lunch at more sporadic times.

Teachers' earlier authority was removed, and their decisions later only concerned their work, student behavior and learning, and their curricular needs. The reins were tightened so that teachers could push and prepare students more efficiently according to district mandates and goals to meet the expectations and needs of the neighborhood schools. By the third year, this way of operating had become standard; because the school was small, the teams of teachers, for the most part, shared students. Not all team members knew all of their students, but they did work together to discuss students' needs. They made this commitment to each other.

During the first year, two of us had been veteran English as Second Language (ESL) teachers of 20 years each and had previously taught second language university students who were preparing to study at American universities. Those students often came from comfortable family backgrounds, and not from marginalized socio-economic backgrounds, as was the case with the majority of the immigrant students at the Newcomer Academy. Serving the language needs of low-language ability adolescent immigrant students and addressing their economic and emotional needs, as well as facilitating their cultural adjustments, were completely different experiences. Despite the years of experience as ESL teachers, the demands were so different that each day was a new challenge; the veterans among us were continually rethinking our ideas of how and what to teach.

Most of the Newcomer Academy students who came from more comfortable economic backgrounds had higher scores on their English tests and went to another high school in another part of town. This school informally called itself the Newcomer Academy because of the diverse population it served. The students at this school did not attend so much by choice as by the fact that their families had settled in this area. Many of these students had studied English in their home country all of their lives; therefore, they were also able to attend a neighborhood high school immediately without the need of extra support. The students at the Newcomer Academy had scored below a third-grade reading level on a statewide test and came from the entire school district for a two-year transitional period and then returned to their neighborhood high school.

During the first two years, professionals held a number of warring positions about how to teach English. The veteran ESL teachers wanted the schools to put more emphasis on the English production and grammar abilities. They wanted to turn at least the first six weeks, if not the first semester, strictly to English language classes. The administration contended that the students did not have enough time to learn English; it suggested that they needed to dive in and start with modified courses, while concurrently taking a reading and a language arts class. The administration held a philosophy I call the border approach because for the most part, the administration had grown up along the border of Texas. They had learned English by going to school, and they argued that these students could learn English that way as well. If the students worked in teams on projects, the good students would serve as mentors or leaders in a group, and the students would learn from each other.

There were several unspoken assumptions underlying the border approach. Students would work in groups. The teachers would understand Spanish and use the language strategically when they gave instructions, and when the students needed encouragement privately. Staff and students would frequently speak Spanish when others were not present, so that its use would not be questioned or raise a challenge that would press the school to declare its policy regarding language use. The school adopted an informal and unofficial secondary bilingual and dual language program when no one was looking. When asked, administrators said it was a program that supported English use through teamwork and exposure to English. When talking with ESL teachers or others, it was a school that taught grammar, even though few could see evidence of it. The tension between ESL teachers and those who practiced the border approach centered on how explicitly language was taught and what kinds of supports were put in place for the students. Of more importance to the practitioners of the border approach was the emotional support that the school offered, which allowed the students to find their own way. The two approaches seemed to fall between two cultures: those who were Euro-American ESL teachers versus those who were Latino and had grown up in the Rio Grande Valley or close to it.

One problematic aspect of the border approach for the language teachers was the apparent lack of realization that these students were arriving as 14- and 15-year-olds and had high demands for performance placed on them. In the second year, the horizontal teams became the dominant teams that functioned at the school. The voice of the English language teachers became only one voice among many, and these teachers were often ignored or seen as holding only one point of view among the subject matter teachers; the focus on the goals of the academic class or the belief in the border approach took precedence.

During the first year of the horizontal teams, the tensions about the approach to be used with the students did not surface in the discussions. Instead, they emerged in the parking lot or privately in classrooms behind closed doors, as those who tried to teach mostly in English and those who used Spanish worked in their own ways without talking about the issue directly. There was a don't ask, don't tell attitude about how to work with the students.

By the third year, all of the hard-core ESL teachers, including myself, were no longer at the school, each for our own reasons. The principal replaced these teachers with young teachers with no ESL background and often no teaching experience, so that she could train them. Thus, although teachers had less authority and autonomy, they felt good about working within their teams because they created a supportive network for each other. They had a fresh attitude and approach because they didn't have any bias one way or another—either for or against ESL, grammar, or border—or they were happy to teach in a school with such responsive students. They were just trying to survive their first year of teaching, which is a challenge in any setting. They offered each other support, and through their collective group wisdom, they created an approach that worked based on their relationships with the students and what they felt the students needed to learn. The younger group of teachers was from a generation more comfortable with teamwork and the team process, in contrast to teachers from past generations, who were accustomed to working alone.

As I worked with this population of students, I became much less of a hard-core ESL teacher and much more a believer in the relationship and supportive approach. I met students in their third year at Stafford High School and was amazed when two students who had absolutely no English ability during their first year studied every morning outside the library and did well in their courses through their combined efforts. These two cousins helped each other make it through high school. Students sometimes spoke haltingly and with broken grammar, but they functioned well enough to pass their classes in school. Ironically, students who might have been more linguistically advanced began to drop out because they needed to work, weren't disciplined or interested in school, had personal distractions such as boyfriends or girlfriends, or any other number of personal issues. Some of those who had begun their journey with limited language ability did well in their classes because, as students at an urban school, their effort and hard work pushed them beyond the performance of their U.S.born, alienated peers. Many research studies have documented the dichotomy between new immigrants and their second- and third-generation cousins (Ogbu, 2008; Olsen, 2008; Valenzuela, 1999).

## Physical Appearance of the School and Neighborhood

The Newcomer Academy was housed in the north wing of the Robert E. Lee neighborhood school building. It was next to the gym, practice field, and the school's childcare center. From the outside, the building looked stark. During the first year, no grass grew on the grounds outside, the playing and practice field for both schools had no bleachers, and the tennis courts were in a state of disrepair. A great deal of construction and renovation took place during the first four years. An elevator was installed, old bathrooms were renovated, the schools underwent a good deal of mold removal, and grass was planted. In general, the school took on a more welcoming appearance from the outside. However, the outside doors of the school were routinely locked until school began, so it was difficult to enter the school except through one inside door. This practice, as in the majority of schools in the United States that attempt to provide a safe school environment, kept unwanted visitors to a minimum. A colorful sign greeted visitors who found the one door that was open.

The look and feel inside the halls of the school was entirely different. Posters and student work hung on every available square inch of space. The halls painted a portrait of a student population that the adults in the building honored and spotlighted. The stairwells were covered with student work and announcements that invited students to participate in activities or projects such as soccer, peer mediation, or Saturday school sessions. When students passed the classroom doors, they liked to peer in at their friends and classmates. Many teachers put pictures of their classes and made collages of the students on the glass panels of the doors, which gave an appearance of many faces looking out. This practice kept the peering students from interrupting other students when classes were in session, and it somehow satisfied their need to see their friends.

## Student and Staff Population Demographics

In the first year, between 280 and 340 students attended at different times during the school year. The initial staff of six teachers expanded to eight after the first six weeks and consisted of a director, a curriculum specialist, two secretaries, a counselor, and a social worker. The curriculum specialist was to work with the students and teachers but was pulled down to the principal's office and instead acted informally as an assistant principal. Toward the end of the first year, the curriculum specialist worked with groups of five or six students during part of the day after much discussion about the need to support low-level students. Two teachers' aides rotated in and out of the classrooms at varying times of the day. The demographics of the student population varied from year to year but were similar in many ways to the first year. Over 90 percent of the students came from Mexico with some representation from El Salvador, Honduras, and other Central American countries (two to four percent), Cuba (three to four percent), and Africa (about two percent). A few Asian students came from Vietnam (one to two percent), and one Russian student attended. In subsequent years, a sprinkling of Myanmar refugee students came, as well as some Japanese and Iranian students. From the third year on, the school hired about 16 to 22 teachers, a principal, and an assistant principal.

## Hall Culture

Usually halls are places where students feel free from the constraints of teachers. They have moments of freedom when they pass from one class to another. We had a sense of how the students felt about the school by how they acted in this somewhat unconstrained setting. When we saw the students in the halls, they showed a vibrancy and camaraderie not seen in other urban schools. The students laughed, joked, and enjoyed each other's company. The artwork and posters displayed on the walls seemed to match the joy of the students passing in the hall. Students walked arm in arm and easily called out to teachers as they passed. Bright student projects seemed to jump off the walls to greet visitors—drawings of cells for a biology class, story lines from an English class, scrolls of a mini-drama created in a social studies class, and pharaoh illustrations wrapped in text, a joint project between a world history and art teacher. The halls of this school were alive, and the students felt valued as they displayed their schoolwork.

## Restructuring Vision and Challenge

Creating the school vision was a challenging process achieved through the collaboration of strategic partners. In the words of Anabel, the principal:

> The first year I was given this task, it was very difficult to decide on a vision and a focus because I came in about five days before school started...I applied some very solid strategies that have worked in different schools. I wanted to establish the "team concept" so that the teachers could support each other and common students and could discuss academic progress, academic problems, or disciplinary problems, communicating with the parents.

With limited feedback from the teachers, the school's restructuring plan evolved in conjunction with an alliance with Stafford High School. The two schools shared consultants, restructuring models, and in general used many of the same strategies to serve this population. I often wondered why the Newcomer Academy campus was not located at Stafford because so many of the students returned there. It would have cut the transportation costs and time in half. It would have helped the large number of immigrant students, and even their second- and third-generation cousins and friends, to have the language and cultural supports in place at their neighborhood school.

## Curriculum and Performance Indicators

In its fourth year, the school received support from three ongoing district consultants. The principal shared these consultants with Stafford High School in a strategic alliance to continue the school's success, especially in the event of Robert E. Lee's closure due to low performance.

The consultants assisted with:

1. Standardized test preparation, in which teachers were trained to teach the state standards that were tested on the state accountability test. That is, they would focus their teaching strategically on the actual teaching points throughout the entire school year that have historically been tested on the state standardized tests;
2. Consultants from the bilingual department, who provided a two-day workshop on how to teach a Sheltered Instruction Observational Protocol (SIOP). This technique was designed to assist with adapting a curriculum for English language learners once the students moved past the basic English skills;

3. A consultant shared with Robert E. Lee, where teachers were trained to identify past, present, and future curriculum gaps in students' preparation of math in an effort to close achievement gaps; and

4. A program developed over two years that involved training a core group of teachers who would continue to work with a consultant and, in turn, train the rest of the staff. Selected teachers would work closely with the consultants, whose purpose was to guide them on how to adapt their teaching for English language learners. This teaching was somewhat like SIOP but was designed to create an ongoing and daily practice of the ESL/content adaptations.

The principals selected these consultants in conjunction with Stafford and Lee High Schools.

English teachers from both Stafford High School and, during the first two years, the Newcomer Academy asked the academy to teach grammar to students; but little time was left for this activity with the focus that the four administrator-chosen models provided. The students were initially exempt from taking the state-mandated tests for the two-year duration of their stay at the Newcomer Academy. Later, however, depending on their circumstances, some students had to take the test in their second year. Results of the history and math tests showed some success, but the students performed poorly on the English tests. They typically performed better on the social studies test because the language arts tests required analyzing complex reading passages. The state placed these high demands on the students even though the majority of them were reading between the third and sixth grade level during the second year. Meeting these state-mandated tests continued to be a challenge, regardless of when the students took the test.

## Concluding Remarks

The Newcomer Academy enjoyed an extremely positive school culture, a team structure to support new teachers, and students who were working to improve their English language skills and adapt to a new culture and school system. Further, the administration and staff were 100 percent Latino, and the teaching staff was largely Anglo (five teachers out of 22 were Latino; one was Taiwanese). The Latino administration, staff, and teaching assistants created a buffer for the students and provided support in their out-of-class experiences. This assistance has proven to be a very important part of the creation of a culture to support the teacher's modifications in the classroom and a positive school setting.

*The Butterfly*

*Trying to hold*
*the ethereal,*
*to pin down*
*butterfly wings,*
*brings death.*

*Regret comes from trying to make permanent*
*the impermanent.*

—Barbara McKinley, *Dear Muse* (1995, p. 36)

# 2

## *The Profiles of Care*

> *at once other (and higher) needs emerge . . .*
> *and when these are satisfied, again new still higher,*
> *and so on . . .*
>
> —Abraham Maslow (1987, p. 17)

Teachers set the tone in a classroom. Students, staff, peers, and administration selected the teachers in this study as those who taught their subject well and were also engaged with their students. The descriptions of how the teachers interacted with their students do not represent a formula or script of what teachers should do or how they should be. Rather, these teachers' narrations of what they thought and what they did give us a glimpse into their classrooms. The stories may have universal appeal; we may see parts of ourselves in these teachers, and in this way, they represent teachers anywhere. The same applies to the principal, staff members, and students. While the teachers affect the school culture, classroom by classroom, it is the principal and the support staff who set the tone for the entire school—and allow their school to be a place where people feel cared for.

*Care & Advocacy: Narratives from a School for Immigrant Youth*, pages 13–28

What follows are short biographical sketches of the teachers, the principal, the older staff members who acted as grandparents (abuelos), and the students themselves—all profiles of care. The following chapters will depict the practice of care, which led them to become advocates for the students. The last chapters define their practice of advocacy for their students. Some of the participants have requested that I use their actual names.

## The Teachers

### *Denise Norris, Science Teacher, Actual Name*

Denise Norris, an Anglo female, was married and had children of her own in high school and beyond. Although she was middle aged with a maternal build and mannerisms, she had fiery red hair and a perky personality to match. She would post herself at her door between classes to greet students and passersby; whenever I walked by her room, she would call out a greeting "Hello, there!" in a voice that was at once inviting and reassuring. Her voice and personality were warm, highlighted with laughter and a sense of humor that invited us into her room. Denise had taught science for more than 15 years in Samuelson public schools. Because she was the first teacher interviewed, she served as a key informant in many ways. She was a peer when I taught at the school where we were founding teachers together, two among the eight teachers who were hired during the school's first days. From that experience, I learned how to keep a focus on curriculum and expectations high.

I interviewed her over the summer before I ever approached the other teachers. Her interviews were more in depth, perhaps because we had worked as peers or because they took place without the constraints of the school day. After her interviews, I was able to refine and refocus my questions for the other teachers. In addition to the interviews, I observed her classes and attended the team meetings at which she presided as team leader. We had shared many experiences, and I felt to be an insider, albeit for the most part, I was clearly an outsider during the research process.

Denise lived in Ohio, Mexico, and New Jersey while growing up. She said she and her siblings would see the moving van in front of their house and knew it was time for another family move.

> I can remember one time, when we moved to Ohio, I had never even seen our house. I went from the hotel to school and took the school bus to where I thought my house would be. I didn't know what it looked like, and unbeknownst to me, the street signs had been switched around. So, I didn't know

where we lived—I looked for the moving vans, which were always a hallmark of our family.

Denise, the oldest of eight siblings, felt that her parents enrolled all of their children in parochial schools as a way to create continuity among their many moves. With their move to Mexico, the family found themselves in a British school system. Denise and her siblings lost most of their credits and were placed last in class rankings. In every class, their grades were publicly ranked in relation to the others in the class. "That was so cruel," she said. "All of us were close to last in each of our classes."

Her positive and upbeat personality may have developed as a result of moving so frequently, and it helped her adapt to the variety of localities as she grew up. She developed flexibility and an ability to roll with the situations. A practice that emerged from these childhood experiences was the importance she gave to welcoming her students and greeting them as they entered her classroom. When students entered at odd times of the year, she helped them feel that they were at home and a part of the class. If students had to leave unexpectedly, she knew how to talk with them because she had an understanding of what it felt like to leave before the end of the school year. Further, her experience in Mexico helped her understand the Hispanic/Latino immigrant students from a cultural and linguistic perspective.

> In Mexico, we lived in apartment buildings. We lived on the ninth and tenth floors in an area with a very intense concentration of people. We got to know a lot of them. We were kids, and everyone was curious about us. We learned Spanish pretty quickly, actually. In fact, we still use a lot of the customs that we got from those years. (We sing) "Happy Birthday" and Christmas songs in Spanish. The way we eat some foods; we always eat our corn with mayonnaise, Mexican style. Stuff like that.

## Jennifer Watson, Art Teacher

Jennifer grew up in a small town and graduated early so that she could get out of there. She had loving parents who provided a stable and caring environment, but Jennifer, as an artist, felt stifled by the religious regimen that her parents imposed. She and her siblings could play with anyone as long as they were from her church; she attended church every night.

> I had resentments from my upbringing because of things I didn't get to experience. My parents took us to church six times a week. (They said,) "This way is the path to be on; you can't stray from it." But I did have good memo-

ries. My mom was a good mom. She liked to celebrate the holidays, and we would always have big Halloween and Christmas parties for the whole neighborhood. There were lots of gatherings and fun stuff at our house, but if an activity was outside of the church group, it wasn't allowed.

As an artist, Jennifer found that she did not fit easily into this mold. Early on, she knew that she would have to find a way to escape. Although school was also not a favorite place ("I was the student they found hiding out under stairwells"), her art teacher and her classroom provided a second home for Jennifer. Once Jennifer realized that she wanted to leave home, she found a way to graduate early.

She attended her junior year classes in the mornings, and then in the evenings went to a self-paced program for her senior year. The program was for the "bad" students who needed credits to finish school. A few took the classes for accelerated study, but for the most part, the other students were recovering credits. She finished her English class in a month, reading and writing without interruption, and then moved on to finish other classes. At 16, she was able to graduate and found that the only university her parents would pay for was a nearby Christian college. This school's environment also became stifling, and she dropped out for a while.

Realizing that she did not want to wait tables all of her life, Jennifer went back to finish school and get a certificate to teach. "I can be the teacher students come to school for," she figured. This belief became a goal for her, and she finished college in a year and a half. She went back to school at the age when many others who started with her would be graduating; her gains from early graduation were lost, but she seemed to have an understanding and purpose that were not there earlier.

### Melissa Arasin, English Teacher, Actual Name

Melissa was a spry, youthful teacher in her first year of teaching. She was saucy, bouncy, and smart. Her erect posture was something I could not help but notice, but she also seemed to be very relaxed and comfortable. Melissa was from a small town an hour's drive from Houston, Texas. The high school she attended had about the same population as the Newcomer Academy (approximately 300 students). With many of the Newcomer Academy students themselves from rural backgrounds, she seemed right at home with them. Melissa talked about having a stay-at-home dad who was a little scary. He was probably bipolar, but that term was not in the popular nomenclature when she grew up. With an unstable home situation, Melissa found school a safe haven. She stayed there as long as she could, arriving early and staying late, until 6 p.m. or so, when her mom picked her up. Melissa stayed with her band director and they talked while they did their work. Their relationship, as well as her relationships with the other band members, kept her in school. Perhaps they also kept her safe.

Melissa remembered acting out a great deal at school. For example, even though she was qualified for the National Honor Society, she felt that a teacher had targeted her as a bad student; this teacher then influenced the others to keep Melissa out of the National Honor Society until her senior year. The teacher may have been influenced by Melissa's dressing in a Goth style. Melissa learned how to make adjustments so that she could feel more a part of the school community. From this experience, she felt that she learned how to work the system at an early age. Her ability to use school as a refuge is part of why Melissa became a high school teacher.

Melissa and Margaret were the only two original teachers still at the Newcomer Academy as this book was written. Melissa remained open both to the students and how to teach them. She realized during her first year that a number of the students needed more language support than the school was able to give or admit the students needed. She persevered and remained close to the students.

### Jesse DelaHuerta, Math Teacher, Actual Name

Jesse grew up close to the Mexico-Texas border. He remembered being outdoors for most of his childhood, playing games of all kinds with the neighborhood kids. His father called him with a whistle when it was time to come home. The kids all knew to get home at the signal, and their parents did not worry about them. The parents actually seemed surprised later when their children told them how far away they had actually played.

At school, Jesse liked to continue his playing; he would often rush to finish his work and then disrupt the other students. The teachers gladly let him roam the halls so that he would not disrupt the class. Jesse was taken aback when he was in the top ten percent of the class and actually close to the top five percent. "There has to be some mistake," he thought. Because he was from a similar background as the students at the Newcomer Academy, he felt that he could understand them. He knew what they were going to say, what excuses they would give, and the way they thought. The students said, "We can't con this guy; he knows what we're going to say before we say it."

Jesse never really liked school and did not want to go to college. His mom cried, which seemed to be enough persuasion, along with the counselor, principal, and parents sitting him down and saying, "Okay, this is how it will be. You've been offered all of these scholarships, and you're going to go to one of these schools." They convinced him to go to college, and he chose the flagship university in the state. His principal took him aside and said, "You know, it's different up there." He implied that Jesse might encounter racism in an Anglo world, which was unlike the largely Hispanic world along the border.

Jesse was a teacher that students always came back to visit because, in his own words, he was always there for them. He had insights on how to work with them because he grew up in similar circumstances. He talked about the students being like cousins, relatives, or family members. This connection was something that the students felt right away. A few years ago, when I was also a teacher, he told me that he never intended to teach. He was going to drive a truck, like his father. By the end of his first year of teaching, he had founded an after-school club for the students and brought buddies from his university fraternity to mentor them. It was pretty apparent that he was hooked and would teach for many years. The students made him want to be a better teacher. He is now in a principalship program at the neighboring university.

## The Principal: Anabel Garza, Actual Name

The principal, Anabel Garza, was raised in the same border town as Jesse. In fact, she went to school with his parents and knew them. She mentored Jesse in his principalship program. Anabel's parents were overprotective, and her mother and father only let her play with family members and children from her church. She could do anything as long as it was at her church, so she was always looking for activities there. She lived in a rough neighborhood, but her parents structured her life so that she would succeed and not get pulled into any negative activities. Like the art teacher, she plotted her escape from parents who both loved and stifled her.

Every year, the family's trips to Mexico to visit relatives in a remote village provided important childhood memories. The relatives lived and worked on a primitive farm without running water. They fed and cared for animals, collected eggs from the chickens, and killed rattlesnakes. These memories stayed with Anabel and they helped her understand the immigrant students from Mexico, along with the fact that she herself came from a border area. The rural environment in Mexico afforded her the ability to run and play more freely than back home.

After graduating from high school, she left home to attend classes with a communications scholarship at the flagship university. She had loved her work as a reporter in high school and had been the editor of the school newspaper. The experience at the university was so different that she stopped going to classes—and dropped out of school. She had to wait a year before returning to school; during that time, she decided to get a teaching certificate because her father had been a middle school teacher and coach. She thought that teaching would be something she could do until she figured out her real interests. She has been teaching all of these years and became the principal at one of the toughest high schools in town.

Anabel set the tone at the Newcomer Academy for acceptance, relationship building, openness, and honesty.

> Going back to your question, can you say you are sorry? I have to deal with these things every day. Last week, we had three boys who were tardy, and I was very upset with them. The teacher had asked them to wait outside the room, but one just got up and left. I started talking with him, and he kept on snickering. So I thought, you know, this student is in trouble! "You call your mother right now, and tell her to get up here right now. Do you *care* about this?" And he goes, "Whatever."

Anabel goes on to tell about how she had really upset the student with this confrontation and eventually she went to their house on Halloween, while she was in her costume, to apologize to the family. It was this kind of openness that set the tone for the school. Denise said, "It was the topic of many conversations among the teachers, and we know that it really did affect her. We respected that; as a faculty, we respected that."[1]

## The Grandparents (Los Abuelitos)

Four members of the Newcomer Academy's staff acted as abuelos, or grandparents, for the students. The computer technician, a teaching assistant, an academic-special projects coordinator, and a school secretary were four people whose relationships with the students far exceeded their official job descriptions.

### *Dario "Marty" Martinez, Terry Villegas, Linda Sue Rodriguez, and Elle Stanley, Actual Names*

The computer technician, whom the students affectionately called Mr. Monster, was a favorite with many students. He would not have been happy being called abuelo, but one of the reasons he especially talked with the students was that he was not able to live with his own children due to a divorce. Even students who had graduated from the Newcomer Academy and moved on to the school down the hall from them stopped by to check in with him when they returned to campus after tennis meets or other off-campus events. Stopping by his office was like checking in with mom when they got home from school.

Dario "Marty" Martinez, or Mr. Monster, had a grey ponytail down his back, segmented by rubber bands every couple of inches down his hair's length, which gave him a Native American look. He was a tough guy who found a place in his heart for the students. He would let them know, in his own words, "where the line was." He did special things for students on his own time, like fixing their computers after hours. He tutored the students who came and asked him for help, and in general was there to tease and chat with them.

The principal had all of the support staff—including secretaries, computer technicians, teachers' aide, and the school registrar—come out into the hall to help students as they passed from one class to another. The students wanted to chat with them, but the group smiled and told them to move on, "Let's go to class." There was a family feeling in the hall rather than a disciplinary tone to the encouragements. Students and adults smiled and moved along.

Teresa Villegas, or Ms. Terry, as the students called her, was also often called Abuela or Abuelita. She, like Mr. Monster, was in the halls and cafeteria with the students. She would sit at a table, and students came by to ask her questions or confide personal details, calling, "Hola, Abuela!" She was the person who taught me how to relate to the students: Be a friend.

One day Ms. Terry could not find her dictionary and asked every student, "Where is my dictionary? Do you know who took it? How can I help you without it?" She made her missing dictionary everyone's problem. She got it back the next day, conveyed to her via the network of students who asked and checked for it.

She went after the rude boys, chased down those who cut in line, and got security guards to come and take students who wouldn't show her what they were hiding in their pockets or lockers. "Sometimes you have to be firm with them, too. They may want to take advantage of you," she advised. She did not take any evasiveness from the students. The more she stood up to them, the more they seemed to love her. They liked it when she got on them. She would tell them, "I want you to succeed...so you can build a swimming pool some day and invite me over...or be a doctor and cure me." She loved to joke with them, and they seemed to like it, too.

She helped the students navigate the school system in that they didn't know how things worked. "They are away from home, and some of them have been raised by grandmas . . . so they see me, and they relate to me as a mother figure, grandma figure."

Linda Rodriguez, another grandmother, or abuela, worked with the principal and teachers on special projects, including testing, finding materials for students who needed extra support, or writing grants. She organized a Ballet Folklorico group for the students the first year so that they could perform in the community. She brought in the costumes, got the students set up, and organized the practices and the places where they performed. She did not know the dances but knew that the students did; they just needed someone who would encourage them to keep these traditions alive. She was persistent with the girls who came to school not quite fully dressed. If they saw her coming over to their table in the cafeteria, they knew to put on the shirt they had tucked in their backpack—either that, or they'd have to put on the oversized T-shirts she had in her office.

Elle Stanley felt that she was an advocate for the students' needs, whether it meant getting dictionaries for everyone or getting backpacks donated by local businesses. She felt that her background with preschool students had prepared her for students who were new to the United States. The new immigrants were in a new country, a new school environment, and were often away from their families. "They are like preschoolers in a 15-year-old body," she commented. She had a personal passion for working with new immigrants because of her grandfather's experience. He wanted to go to school but was not allowed to because he did not speak English. His story created her determination to help students succeed.

When students were going to be absent from Ms. Rodriguez' seminar class, she expected them to call her. "This is like your job," she told them. "If you cannot come to class, or you are going to be out, then you need to call me and let me know." She gave them her cell phone number as well as the classroom phone number, so they could reach her directly. They did call her.

Ms. Stanley, a staff member who kept records and arranged for the substitute teachers, helped the students in special ways from the very beginning. She also provided a warm, maternal figure for the students and families. She processed the paperwork for the students to get their free or reduced lunches. For her, this job was more than paperwork because she knew that when the paperwork was filed, the students could start eating at school. The students stayed with her when they felt sick, so her office doubled as the school infirmary. She also helped them figure out the buses for getting home. All of these were routine office tasks, but the way that Ms. Stanley interacted with the students and the way they responded by coming by to hang out made her office feel like home. She had snacks if they were hungry and listened if they had something to say. She played grandma and usually had a giggle for the teenagers.

A strong sense of family prevailed in the way that the staff responded to the students and their needs. If students came to the staff for help, their requests were honored and respected. These special requests possibly took precedence over academic needs.

Comments from these staff members showed that they felt a connection with both the school and the students: "I love my job," or "I wouldn't be anywhere else," or "I look forward to coming to work every day." They bonded with the students so naturally that the students sought them out. They were an important part of what Campano (2007) called the second classroom, or the hallway and out-of-classroom places where students congregate at school. These staff members had their official job titles, but the students came to them with special needs in the same way that they came to their moms or family members—and they were treated that way by the staff.

## The Students

As a teacher, I knew and had contact with many students from the Newcomer Academy over the four years of my research. Enrollment in my reading classes reached 140 students. The following year, which was the junior year for those students who entered the Academy in its first year, I taught at Stafford High School, which was the neighborhood school for the majority of the Newcomer Students. I became an advisory teacher for about five of the students during their junior year, and my classroom was a place where they could visit. I also taught Newcomer Academy students who had chosen to remain at the neighborhood school in lieu of attending the Newcomer Academy. My contact during the fourth year was occasional, as I only returned to interview specific students for the research. Some of the students have kept in touch with me and are friends on Facebook. Comments from other students who were interviewed in passing or only for a few minutes may also be included in the study.

### Jon, a Student from Pakistan

Jon is a Pakistani student from Larkarna, the same city as Benazir Bhutto. He moved to another city, Sadiqabad, when he was in fifth grade, and at the same time, his dad moved to the United States. His family moved in with relatives and only came to the United States three years ago, when he was 16 years old. "We didn't have to come. My father just wanted us to have a better chance at education," he said. When Jon thought back to his childhood, he thought about his grandfather. Of all of his relatives, his grandfather was the closest to him, and his fondest memories were of being with his grandfather.

He lost his first two years of high school when he came to the Newcomer Academy as a freshman and graduated a year later than he would have in Pakistan. He planned to attend a university in Texas and wanted to study medicine. Jon had a sense of humor and was often playful in class. Sometimes, when I was teaching, I would look up and Jon would just be sitting in my classroom. He must have had a hall pass to go the bathroom from another class and would just stop by for a break. He liked to tease the girls, perhaps because he did not speak Spanish, and most of them did. He learned early how to say hola, or hello, in Spanish and other conversation starters. He studied Spanish for three years in school and would have been in the fourth year, except that class was only for native speakers.

After the first year, he left the Newcomer Academy but then returned suddenly to complete the second year at the transitional high school. There are two versions of the story of why he attended the Newcomer Academy for two years. One is that his parents wanted him to come back to the more sheltered environment there. He had attended his neighborhood school for a couple of weeks, but an incident spurred his parents to send him back. Another story was that his sister was attending the Newcomer Academy, and he wanted to stay with her. They both left the Newcomer Academy when he advanced. In other words, she exited a year before she needed to, and they both attended Stafford for two years together.

As a graduating senior, he worked as an office aide during the last period of the day. As such, he often helped me find students when I needed to talk with them. He was tall, handsome, and active in school. He joined the Asian Club and was a member for two years. He wished he had learned about community service and being active in school activities sooner but conceded that maybe he would not have really done anything before his junior year, anyway.

Jon later attended the community college in town.

## Olivia, a Student from Monterrey, Mexico

Olivia was an amazingly articulate student from Monterrey, Mexico. From her childhood, she remembered playing soccer outside with her neighborhood friends. She had been in the United States for three years when I met her. What struck me was not only her command of the English language, but also her self-awareness and confidence. She thanked her English teacher right away for spending extra time with her to help her learn English. When she came to the U.S., she only knew how to say the colors. Over the past three years, many of her teachers had encouraged her. Olivia left Mexico for a better life and will most likely go to the university after she graduates from high school; however, she may also return to Mexico for family reasons. She was considering her options.

Olivia conveyed a sense of the complexity of the decisions she had to make. She had to decide among three state universities. As she reviewed the options, it struck me that she did things in a methodical, mature manner and realized the implications of each of the choices. It was hard to remember she had not yet graduated from high school. Perhaps she learned to weigh her alternatives when she was in Mexico, for her parents would advise her that some friends were not good influences for her. She considered what her mother told her, understood what she had cautioned about, and followed her mom's advice. "I went to different elementary schools when I was little. I had to change my friends from time to time because some weren't really good for me. My parents told me sometimes that a friendship was not appropriate." For whatever reason, Olivia displayed an unusual maturity.

Olivia attended the flagship university after graduating.

### Raul, a Student from Guanajuato, Mexico

Raul was from Guanajuato, Mexico. He had been in the U.S. for four years and was due to graduate from high school. Raul was in my class two years previously and was an extremely outgoing student who liked to tease people, going a little too far, sometimes. He used to come into my class routinely and open the overhead projector, turn off the bulb inside, and wait for my reaction. After the second time, I learned to open the overhead routinely and turn the bulb back on. He was used to throwing his teachers off, but for some reason, I enjoyed his peskiness. I used to say to him, "I am not a teacher," and he would reply, "And I am not a student." He was an intense presence in the classroom, and when he was absent, I found myself missing my *pretend* adversary. Other teachers may have been glad he was absent. He promised me that he would graduate, but he could not promise to stay out of trouble. He said, "I will try, but it is hard not to get in trouble, even if there are consequences."

When he lived in Mexico, he would ride his bike to a remote village to visit his grandparents on weekends. He lived with his parents in the U.S. He remembered that in Guanajuato, Mexico, the children would play together every day after school. "I used to walk outside my house, and there I would see all these kids having fun. That is something I just don't see here at all." Lots of kids played around in the neighborhood. His house was much bigger in Mexico, compared to the one here, and each of the children had his own room.

Raul went on to study computers at a local vocational college.

### Martine, a Student from Honduras

Martine was articulate in a thoughtful and reflective way. His manner of speaking seemed highly confidential and valuable. I was never his teacher, but he would always take time to greet me. One day when I was looking for him, he appeared out of nowhere, on crutches after an injury in a football game. He had played soccer all of his life, and football may have been a little rough for him at first, especially as he played on a team that did not have depth in its bench. The last time I went to interview him, he was looking for a quotation from Shakespeare for his senior English class. He read about Hamlet and his dilemma: "Will he become evil if he chooses to fight evil?" I liked being able to talk with him about these deep issues even though his English was limited.

The students seemed comfortable communicating in English during their fourth year and spoke fluently and naturally in contrast to their first or second year. It would be easy to think that they were native to the United States. In fact, many teachers stopped thinking of them as newcomers because they were verbally fluent. Somehow, once they had exited the newcomer programs, schools assumed that they would not have any more language-learning issues. Many of the students still needed support with their reading, listening, note taking, and writing.

Martine was trying to get a sports scholarship in soccer or football. He had turned in several applications to various colleges, but he was waiting on his SAT scores. Because he was not in the top ten percent, the flagship university would not automatically accept him. He planned to continue to try to get into a college with his soccer or football abilities and did play soccer for a local university.

He told me that his grandmother had always been important to him. She taught him to initiate relationships with adults and to be respectful, as well as humble: "Do the right thing. Be around the right people." His grandmother raised him until he left Honduras. He left when he was 12 to be with his mother, who had come to the United States when he was four.

### Eduardo, a Student from Cuba

Eduardo came from Cuba and graduated after three years in the United States. He attended the flagship university after his graduation and returned to help students at the Newcomer Academy twice weekly. He was a challenging student to teach because he was extremely smart and advanced in English. He could not sit still. He was one of the first students to be called in for a conference when the teachers started working in teams. Five or six teachers asked him to come in after lunch. They asked him if he knew why they wanted to talk with him, and he said "No." They proceeded to tell him, "We like you, but..." It is very likely that no one had ever talked with him like this before. He registered no emotion that day. Even though Eduardo graduated early, despite his transition to a new country, he did not seem to be excited about being able to attend a top ten percent university. He had no reaction at all. He told me that if he went into his emotions, he might not come out. He preferred to live in the present and move forward.

He was here with his immediate family, but the extended family remained in Cuba. When asked why his father came to the United States, he said that it was too complex to explain. The reasons were personal, political, and professional. He did not let himself miss his extended family because he wanted to succeed in the present. "I forget easily. I focus on what I am doing now," he said. "If I start thinking about all of the past, it will affect my development."

In Cuba, Eduardo liked playing outside and was often in the water; a river was near his house. He and all of the other neighborhood children played outside, too. He may have had homework, but he said, "It wasn't a priority."

### Alicia, a Student from Guanajuato, Mexico

Alicia and I immediately bonded because of her love of poetry. She used to copy poems from a book, and we put the poems on a poster board for the classroom. She was private in many ways but did not lack confidence. When she moved to another city, she used to email me often and talked about how hard it was. She was in a predominantly Anglo school setting and felt isolated. It was her sense that the teachers were racist. When I asked her about that feeling recently, she said she later realized that the teachers had corrected her papers so much to help her learn, not because they were racist. She seemed to have matured and learned to look upon her situation differently.

Alicia used to spend much of her free time with Americans, but in her senior year, she spent her free time with friends from Mexico. The American students wanted to skip and cut classes, so they no longer held much appeal for her. Finding a true friend was more important to her than having many friends. She was not worried about having a boyfriend, and as we interviewed, her Mexican girl friend was waiting for her.

Alicia did not have any concrete plans to go to the university after high school. In fact, she thought about going back to Mexico to be with her grandmother, for they might not have time to be together later. Alicia's grandmother raised her until she came to join her dad in the United States three years ago. Alicia felt that she had been old all of her life. She had to grow up quickly because her father left when she was three, and she did not know where her mother was. She had known sadness in her life, but she had a strong spirit. She kept pushing herself in a positive direction.

She came to the U.S. when she was 15. She had dropped out of school and felt that no one loved her. She had been scared to come to the U.S. to meet her dad, whom she had never seen. They began a relationship through telephone conversations, and soon she decided to join him for a new life.

> When I first hugged him, I had never felt before what I experienced then. Every day, he checked on me, how I was doing. All of this was a new feeling for me, and I wanted to do my best, to get his attention. There was someone who cared for me.

Alicia worked as a waitress but talked about being a nurse.

## Martha, a Student from Ethiopia

Martha was from Ethiopia, and I knew her for four years. Any time she was interviewed, her sister, who was about a year younger and a bit shy, sat with her and listened. Her sister would smile but rarely said anything. She was fine with staying in the shadows and letting Martha speak for her. Martha's sister mostly smiled and communicated eloquently with her eyes. Martha had the classic beauty of an Ethiopian, with a quiet, natural elegance and flow to her gait. In advisory class, where I taught her in the junior year, she was one of the students who used that time to do her homework. Everything took her a lot longer to do, and she worked at it until she finished, often working through her lunch. She put a great deal of time and effort into her studies.

My daughter had visited Ethiopia, and when she spoke with Martha and her sister, the two of them opened up more than at any other time. She was very private about her experiences. She mentioned that she had lived with some family members for five years in Kenya as a refugee, for instance. She never talked about her past. Like Eduardo, she seemed to want to keep it there.

She did say, though, that she missed the many social interactions in the Ethiopian culture. The families did many things together with the extended family, the villagers, and neighbors. Martha noticed that people in the United States were often alone. "We do everything alone here."

Schools in Ethiopia started early in the morning at 7 or 8 a.m. The teachers moved from one class to another, and the 40 or 50 students stayed in the same classroom in much the same way as the students do in Pakistan and Cuba. The students remained together and created a cohort that helped each other in school. Martha said that the students were respectful and listened to the teachers. Martha did not pass the state-mandated test and had to complete it before she graduated. I have not spoken with her since then.

*One, withdrawn and*
*private, carries*
*the burden of her parent's*
*chaotic life, inside.*

*The other, belligerent.*
*He carries his parent's chaos*
*outside.*

*In this classroom, these two*
*students meet.*

—Barbara McKinley, *Second Verse* (2006, p. 39)

# 3

## Why is the Care Ethic Important?

### Making the Invisible Visible

*We see with our heart, and not with our eyes.*
—fortune cookie

This study of an urban school experience is based on and embedded in the care ethic as Noddings defined (1984, 1995, 1996, 2002, 2003, 2005), Valenzuela articulated for the Latino population (1999), and Reyes, Scribner, and Scribner contextualized in a school-wide perspective (1999). The relational aspect of the care theory attempts to put into words the mysterious quality or process that takes place between teachers and students. Much has been written about these relationships in the care theory; in fact, much of the literature deals with the complex makeup and necessity of relationships we experience as humans. Some organizations say it takes caring adults to touch a youngster's life to keep itgoing in a positive direction (see, for instance, the website for the organization America's Promise at www.americaspromise.org or Every Child, Every Promise in Dubuque, IA at www.everychild-everypromise.org). A caring adult can help a youngster navigate

*Care & Advocacy: Narratives from a School for Immigrant Youth,* pages 29–38
Copyright © 2012 by Information Age Publishing
**29**

past the rough terrain of street life, or spark an imaginative leap into the future by showing where a road exists to someone who didn't even know there was a road. A yearning for a person to care, recognize our worth, and direct our potential is a driving force in the human condition.

It is through this frame and lens that this study has been carried out.

At present, the care literature has deep theoretical roots in teaching, curriculum, and learning, developed through Noddings' *Philosophy of Care* (1984; 2003), and knowledgeable veteran teachers discuss the awareness of it in their educational circles. This study views the caring relationship and bond that exists between teachers and their students as a means of crossing over a border, especially a border caused by race, class, and ethnicity or the border from failure to success. These borders are inevitably crossed in the quest for social and moral justice and span far beyond any school wall or other barrier. This powerful force between caring individuals in a school can create a glue and environment where students want to stick their hope. This study looks at how one school worked to create this kind of environment across the campus, moving among teachers, classrooms, courses, subjects, and support staff to create a contextualization for *care*, embedded in a school-wide perspective. The narratives that are shared give readers insights into the role school leadership can play in changing the tone and culture of a school, which is inevitable if the focus is truly on the well being of the children.

Indeed, it is through the deep and caring relationships that develop in a school setting that the social, moral, ethical, and critical justice and evolution of a culture begin and take shape. These relationships are at the very core and foundation of social justice, in which a community attempts to create a safe space for its participants to relate through respect, dignity, and empowerment. The narratives from this school tell of how teachers and students, principals and social workers, teacher's aides, and computer technicians pulled together to create a community of support and learning that created and built social capacity and capital in a school setting. Their anecdotes give a face to the theoretical notion of care; they show what care looks like in a school setting and how it forms the basic cornerstone of human development and learning. These contextualized, first-hand narratives extend the care literature to the daily practice and experience of care and feeling cared for.

When school leadership wants to bring about a true transformation in a school culture and social setting, the students, rather than setting fires in bathrooms (Cushman, 2005), will feel that the fire has been set inside of them. Caring relationships help maintain and build the fire that drives just and sustainable school change. The relationships built within a school help connect the school to the community at large and, in this way, transform the community it serves. This is the beginning of social change and true metamorphosis in the course of a school, a community, but most importantly, a child.

## An Anecdote Relating to the Care Ethic in Practice

Caring has traditionally been a concern of teaching, or so Noddings told us (2003). When my mother passed away in December 2004, I was just beginning this study. I didn't initially make a connection between her passing away and my research, but certain events have made this relationship obvious to me now. On the same day of my mother's passing, one of my high school students also died as a result of a car accident. My students and I mourned together. As I reflected, I began to see some rather subtle, yet obvious, connections between my study and these two people who had passed on, and who affected me personally and professionally.

The main concern from my reflections emerged: Why is it important to study the ethic of care, and what is its value to schools? Does it affect performance? If it does, how do we measure its effect? Finally, if care does matter, how is it practiced? When trying to analyze the subtle aspects of schooling that are often nonverbal or highly subjective in nature, we tend to shy away from including them in our discussions; yet, if we ask teachers why they entered the profession, their responses usually relate to the intangible, transformative aspects of teaching. If a student drops out, it can have as much to do with the lack of connection with the school as with the student's personal or financial concerns.

In a culture that respects action, doing, and results, simply being there for someone is sometimes not recognized as doing something important. Creating a safe and inviting space for students can also be an important part of being there. My goal as a teacher at the Newcomer Academy was to create a space that would feel like a second home to my students. We had several round tables, covered with warm green tablecloths. I had covered the windows with sheer, golden curtains that let the sunshine through; they imbued the classroom with their warm color and also allowed the students to look out at the trees. The students' artwork, poetry, class papers, and drawings filled every inch of wall space. Even though my students' parents had never set foot into this classroom, the room felt like a home to the students. It was important for me to make them feel comfortable in the school. We always had music of some kind playing in the background. Some staff members walked by and commented that the classroom was nicer than their own home. I had a corner table where our advisory class could make hot chocolate and oatmeal if they hadn't had breakfast that morning. Creating this ambiance for the students was important for me, and more importantly, for them as well.

The Newcomer Academy served immigrant adolescent students who had scored at a third-grade reading level or less on a placement test. They had the option of attending their neighborhood school and taking their chances with the supports in place there, or they could attend this school with a peer group who shared similar language learning and acculturation issues. At the end of their two-year stay, the students would then transition back to their neighborhood school as juniors with a stronger command of language, successful experiences within the school system, and more positive expectations in their new country.

These students had been pulled from their home country as adolescents by their parents' dream or necessity, which the students might not have completely understood. Many were in the United States for a better life, whatever that meant. They left family and friends behind. In many cases, family meant their grandparents, who had raised them while their parents made a fresh start in the United States; or it meant leaving parents and coming to live with aunts and uncles while their family made the transition to the U.S. as finances and time would allow. These were students whose family bonds were stretched far and wide. Although they were strong at this particular time in their lives, they were vulnerable from this move to a new, sometimes brusque culture and from the especially big hurdle of learning in a new language and immediately functioning in their new surroundings.

My bond with these students was deep, but my understanding of why I felt this connection with them only developed as I found out more about their lives through the in-depth interviews and continued contact with them over a period of time outside of the classroom as a researcher. As a child, my rural parents had moved my family to an affluent area because the school district was the best in town, and we were going to have the best education. We moved there to have a better life. I began to realize that many of the students with low reading levels had come from rural areas of Mexico or Central America and had left to escape severe poverty. Parents in situations like these often fail to consider what the social life, personal perception, and identity of the student will be when she comes from a family without the financial means of her peers. The conspicuous wealth and consumption of others, as Thorstein Veblen noted (2008), can be an education of its own as a child watches the nonchalant privileges of others. My sense of feeling inadequate in my school environment was something I shared with some of my students. This awareness may not have been conscious; it is apparent more in the way we are received than something we can articulate in our own mind—especially if these values or perceptions are not the ones we receive in our home setting.

My students shared more connections. Reading and writing had been difficult for me, as well. When I was in second grade, I could no longer read the blackboards, and in third grade I could not read the books because of a congenital eye condition. I had operations on my eyes, which put me in the hospital from Thanksgiving until Christmas during third grade. I came back to school with the ability to read street signs and books for the first time, but also with such strange glasses that the children made fun of me. My teacher, Ms. Hill, ran up to me one day, put her arms around me, and said, "We don't care what you look like. We're so happy to have you back!" Throughout my school days, I had times of good vision, but at other times, vision that I could not rely on. In 6th, 10th, and 11th grades, and then again later in college, I had to have operations to be able to see, and I always had to wear thick glasses.

I attended a high-performing, affluent school and was integrated into the *regular* classes—and even attended advanced placement classes—but as far as I can remember, Ms. Hill was one of the only teachers who acknowledged my feelings directly. Many of the teachers seemed either rude or acted as though they were completely unaware of my needs. I felt brave enough to tell one teacher, "I can't read the print on this test." She very loudly told me in front of the class, "Well, if you can't read it, then I'll have to read it for you." I finished the test without her help, as her broadcasting my deficiency made me feel naked in front of all of those, in my mind, very well cared-for and accomplished students. My results on that test had to be thrown out, as they were declared invalid by the testers.

Teachers must have spoken with my parents, but they never gave me that sudden and unexpected hug. In fact, I wasn't voted into the National Honor Society in high school my senior year, even though I was in the top quarter of the class and eligible. This experience made me wonder: How many of the second language learners feel frustrated because they can't read the textbooks that the school expects them to read in English?

This experience of frustration was something I also shared with my students. My first schooling had been in France. My sisters attended the American school, while I walked with my neighbors to the French kindergarten. As the only English speaker, I was often challenged and frustrated. I cried and threw fits because my teacher didn't allow me to do things my mother had asked me to do. For example, my mom had told me to go to a neighbor's house after school, but the teacher required that an adult come pick me up. I often felt pulled between the conflicting instructions of my mother and the school and didn't know how to escape the problem. These past experiences had been tucked away into the deep recesses of my psyche, as I imagine they will be for many of my students. On the surface, I was an academic success story; I graduated, went to college, and started a family of my own.

When I became a parent, I inadvertently put my own children in similar situations. I left California after a difficult divorce for a better life for them in Texas, close to my family and friends. Two of my daughters were adolescents, and like some of my adolescent immigrant students, they wanted nothing to do with the new school or new state. With time, they have understood that the move was necessary and better for us, but it didn't make those first years any easier for them.

On many levels as a child, a parent, and teacher, I empathized and connected with the adolescent immigrant students without completely knowing why, or without talking about it. I intuitively understood that they were strong, but vulnerable; had pride, but needs; had a struggle, but felt compelled to work through the issues on their own without being babied. I also knew that they needed the space, with invisible support to make this growth in their own way. They were in a complex situation without knowing why or really being able to explain it. It has taken me decades to be able to articulate these feelings. It was important that my relationship with my students was strong, so that as they moved into unexpected or difficult situations, I could notice and help them in a way that protected their pride and need for dignity.

Creating a sense of family and home in the classroom was something I did as much for myself as for them. If I was going to spend most of my day there, I wanted it to be an inviting and comfortable environment. One week, I took pictures of my students, one by one and in groups of twos and threes, to put around the upper border of the classroom walls. Their faces staring down from the four walls created a comforting mirror in the classroom. The students made a collage of their faces that we used to cover the glass in our classroom door, so that when people tried to peer in, they saw our faces staring back at them without interrupting our learning. Our plan succeeded in all but one of the classes. In that class, something strange happened to our pictures.

During the same week that I had taken the pictures of my students, I had also taken pictures of my mother and father to share with relatives, as my parents were both in their 90s. When the pictures were returned, it turned out that the film had become double-exposed. The pictures of my mother had become superimposed upon the pictures of my students (see Appendix E for an example of one picture).

Her image was floating in the classroom and blended in with my students. The window behind her bed matched and aligned with the door of my classroom in these pictures. The students, books, flowers, and door in my classroom joined with her bed, pictures on the wall, and the window behind her. It took me a while to figure out what had happened. It was especially curious because my mother was someone who had retreated and let others shine in front of her. In these pictures, she loomed as a central figure, but at the same time, she retreated in a soft but commanding manner due to the faintness of her image.

I didn't want to disappoint my students, but I also didn't know if they would appreciate their pictures the way they were. The pictures stayed in my desk for about a week. And then one day, my sister called me. She said that I needed to come—that my mother was dying. She was 91 years old and had been bedridden for a few months. The next morning, I explained to the class that I would be gone for a while because of my mother. Because I would be gone, I showed them the pictures and explained why I hadn't shared them before. My mom was there in my classroom with us and perhaps had been trying to communicate with me in some remote way I showed the pictures to my amazed students.

They found themselves in these pictures, joined with her. Some were sitting with her. Some seemed to be talking with her. Perhaps they were comforting her. My students showed me that my dad was also hidden deep in some of their faces. One of those students was very, very quiet, and when he saw my dad's face embedded in his, we were joined in a quiet and unspoken way forever. I was joined with my students through these photos in a way that could not be articulated, and none of us tried.

One student, Juan, always sat at the back of the classroom. During the times I thought he was attentive, often he was drawing. Juan's photograph depicts him poised over one of his drawings. He gave us a picture to hang in the classroom, a scorpion with the motto (or warning): ¡No te olvides de México! (Don't forget Mexico!). It was Juan who died in the car accident during the wee hours of the morning—leaving just moments before my mom also passed away. Just that morning, Juan had seen the photo in which he and my mother were in the picture together. It was almost as though she were protecting me—and all of the students, and I guess, especially, Juan. I also could say that she was connected to my students in a way that was beyond time, space, and words—our normal medium for communicating.

Or was it different from the "normal" ways that teachers and students communicate in classrooms? After these pictures were taken, I began reading about the care theory. Little by little, the memory of the pictures crept back. I began to equate the pictures with the ways that teachers and students connect; Michele Foster and colleagues called it a mysterious quality (Foster, Lewis, & Onafowora, 2005). My mother was a gardener, so I could use the metaphor of gardening to describe how she had surfaced in the classroom. We sometimes talk about teaching as a performance, and about improving student performance, but are teaching and learning only about performance? Or, put another way, what causes that performance and motivates a student to learn?

When we put a seed in the ground and watch it grow, is the seed performing? Or is the seed just doing what is natural for it to do—being a seed? Has the gardener, or farmer, done anything? The gardener has prepared the ground, bought the seed, planted, weeded, and watered it. There is some artistry as to which seed to buy, perhaps, or when and how to plant it. But when it comes to growing, the planter has to stand back, wait, and watch while the seed does its thing. Once planted, it takes on a life of its own and will grow in its own way, according to its own direction and natural inclination. We can't get inside that seed and change it, once it's in the ground.

My grandfather was a seed farmer and hybridized seeds; he played with them before they were put in the ground, so that the seed had a good chance of surviving in the dry, dustbowl-sandy soil of southwestern Kansas. In this way, we can say that the internal mechanisms can be adjusted or touched in some way by a careful teacher and observer. Scientists now say that even our DNA, and the brain itself, can change from the effect of a positive attitude (Hamilton, 2009). Teaching that goes beyond our mere words in a lesson allows a teacher to enter a student's thinking or inner mechanism and change some of the internal wiring. The teacher can inspire a student to follow boldly after hunches or to think and express with new confidence. A teacher, in following a student's interest, can join with that student in an incredible journey for both of them. Noddings said that the student who feels cared for will glow and grow (2003).

Alternately, if we use the seed as a metaphor for ideas that can take hold in students, we can see that the seed or idea will connect with the students when they are ready. If we followed the advice of my mom, we would know that some seeds will be carried by the wind; some, the birds will get; and some will be washed away by the rain. The gardener casts only a few of the original seeds that actually grow. We can see the patience and persistence needed in this task of teaching and learning—for a tiny seedling of an idea to take hold in a student's fertile mind is the result of many elements coming together.

These questions and thoughts come to mind when we talk about students' performance, and for that matter, about the performance of teachers. How do we measure this invisible performance? We measure the height of a corn stalk, the yield of a raspberry bush, the size of a melon. Is that how we measure the seed's performance? Is that its outcome? So much depends on so many things. The poet William Carlos Williams said: "So much depends on a red wheelbarrow..." (1985, p. 56). Noddings said that teachers will bend rules and perform in ways that appear irrational to an outside observer, but the student will understand the performance (2003).

And yet these variables that cannot be measured, and that sometimes cannot be controlled, go into the makeup of the measurable results. These invisible, intangible elements are what result from a caring attitude. In the course of time we can see that these intangibles can become part of research about caring teachers, transformational leaders, and schools that create a space for care to develop.

Perhaps my mother's image floating in the classroom has some significance. Perhaps it's a reminder that a teacher's or a mother's work may appear invisible, but it can be so powerful, in a soft and commanding way, so as to even appear or manifest in a daughter's classroom. It can be a strong enough bond to transcend what we know of time, space, and other natural barriers—barriers we take for granted. This caring can even usher a student into his next existence. A mother can reach past time into a need that her daughter has in helping a student let go. A student who never wanted to leave Mexico is taken back to be buried there. ¡No te olvides de México! It can serve to remind us that this caring is strong, powerful, and most importantly, necessary.

It is what connects us—one to another. This study, then, dedicates itself to this spirit, to that quality, force, or push that is in us all to connect and be human in the best way imaginable. In that heartfelt way, we push toward connection, growth and completion. These are the transcendent moments that make teaching worthwhile. As I started the final versions of my study, my father also passed away. My parents' crossing across that border beyond life guided me on this journey to the next stage of my life—and helped my students cross borders of their own.

*Blossoms*

*Like her, I*
*bury my*
*wishes deep.*
*They burst out sudden*

*as the giant mass*
*of yellow roses,*
*sprayed onto the front-yard Mesquite*
*overnight in early Spring.*

*From him, I learned*
*quick insights,*
*bashful but propelling,*
*pushed up and out*
*like a kite in a March wind*
*bound and forced to fly on high.*

*His spirited victory,*
*the impetus for*
*her billowed blossoms*
*springing forth.*

*for my father and mother,*

—Barbara McKinley, *Song of the Suburbs* (2001, p. 7)

# 4

## *The Practice of Care*

*Success in dealing with people
depends on a sympathetic grasp
of another person's viewpoint.*

—Dale Carnegie (1982, p. 162)

The care ethic is a term that has grown out of the philosophical considerations of Noddings (1995, 2003, 2005) and has evolved over various
other strands and fields of study that include philosophy (Mayeroff, 1971;
Noddings, 2003), psychology (Baker-Miller, 1976; Gilligan, 1982), theology
(Buber, 1965, 1966; Macmurray, 1990), sociology (Bellah, Madsen, Sullivan, Sidler, & Tipton, 1985; Valenzuela, 1999), education (Goldstein, 1997,
2002; Noddings, 1995), educational administration (Beck, 1994; Beck &
Murphy, 1994; Marshall & Anderson, 1995; Noblit, 1993; Rusch & Marshall,
1995; Sergiovanni & Starratt, 2002; Sernak, 1998), and health care (Gordon, Benner, & Noddings, 1996; Tarlow, 1996). Noddings's work and discussions are seminal, as they cross several of these fields. For education,
she wrote a strong introductory statement in 1984 that outlined, defined,
and discussed caring as a relational framework. In her first book and in the

*Care & Advocacy: Narratives from a School for Immigrant Youth*, pages 39–52
Copyright © 2012 by Information Age Publishing
**39**

many that followed, Noddings discussed and theorized about the nature and practice of care and caring—or the development of relational aspects in schools, which extend into the community.

It is possible to blend *the care ethic* with theories that examine institutional and organizational constraints (Scott, 2001; Sernak, 1998) or those that look at the barriers school bureaucracies and hierarchical environments create (Blasé & Anderson, 1995; Murphy, 2000; Sergiovanni & Starratt, 2002). Reciprocity (Noddings, 2005), or the notion of caring-with, characterizes care relationships. School governance has often been defined in terms of power relations such as power over, power through, or power with. Blasé and Anderson (1995) described the way that relationships developed among adults at a school site and between adults and their students. This terminology can help school leadership and teachers consider whether they actually create caring relationships, which encourage connections to the school and to each other.

Hierarchical bureaucracies often characterize school structures and environments (Noblitt, 1993; Sernak, 1998). A traditional school environment encourages hierarchical or *power over* relationships (Blasé & Anderson, 1995) between adults and students. For students to feel empowered, or cared for, adults usually adopt a *power through* relationship in which the student works through the teacher's vision, for example. Even more to the point, power sharing or *power with* relationships are the ones that Noddings described as truly relational. One of the most compelling arguments for collaborative, power with relationships in a school, besides the way in which they enhance learning, is the way the participants feel. These kinds of relationships encourage a feeling of confirmation in the student; that is, the student feels cared for (Noddings, 2003, 2005) and will glow and grow.

This chapter focuses on the practice *of care*; that is, on relationships that exist in a *caring with* or *caring through* form. When we consider how much time is spent at school, we can see that it is worth making such a beneficial endeavor. Students, teachers, and administrators spend at least eight hours a day or more, five days a week at school. When we add the commute time to school, extracurricular activities, and homework demands, we can see that the experience of school is an important part of the day for both students and educators alike. Despite this importance, studies of school districts have shown that many high school students in urban schools are being retained in the ninth grade because they do not pass high-stakes testing (Swanson, 2008; Valenzuela, Fuller, & Vasquez-Heilig, 2006), or they exhibit other indicators of poor school performance. Dropout rates, grade retention rates, and low test scores have shown that the high school experience, for multiple reasons, does not resonate with many urban, immigrant students.

If we look at the data from large urban schools, it becomes evident that the typical school experience is more like an unhappy or dysfunctional family. Students may fail for such diverse reasons as economic pressures, familial responsibilities, a sense of disengagement, or language-learning issues. Their challenge is like climbing a difficult mountain without the perceived support of educators, or with any number of peer distractions or circumstances. Each student's personal reason is often recorded in misleading, inaccurate, or only partially true ways in the school records. The real reason for a student's disappearance is not always apparent to school personnel.

In similar ways as their students, teachers in urban schools have found little satisfaction in the experience of teaching. This fact holds true, especially, for those who are young and novice. Studies on teacher retention have given a number of reasons why teachers leave (Darling-Hammond, 2003b; Ingersoll, 2001a; Wilson, Floden, & Ferrini-Mundy, 2001) and have confirmed that many teachers do not feel a connection with their work. Whether it is because of a lack of respect from students, lack of administrative support, the workload, or low pay, teachers are dropping out at alarming rates as well. The real reasons may not always be recorded, just as with the students.

Teacher salaries make up a significant portion of a school's budget. A school administrator must make countless decisions in a single day; perhaps one of the most important decisions will be who to hire. It can take four or more years for a principal to change a school culture through staff development or hiring practices. Perhaps one of the most important responsibilities is the selection of a staff that will create positive learning experiences for students in the school. Students far outnumber any of the staff in a school. If teachers and students, who represent the largest populations at schools, are happy with their environment, then many of the issues we associate as leadership challenges could be resolved. The creation of a positive school environment, culture, and learning community can only occur when the majority of the people's needs are being served.

This chapter shares the experiences of four teachers who served as key informants, and secondarily, those of their teammates. In addition, administrators and support staff are included in the conversation and show their roles in the development of teacher-student relationships and the ethic of care. Their responses convey the importance of these relationships for the overall school design, functioning, and culture.

Seven alumni of the Newcomer Academy and several of their classmates speak about the experience for students. In addition to the students' memories, the memories teachers have of their favorite teachers became an important source of information about the students' perspective of care. The author's memories of teaching these students are also included to triangulate and support the narrations of the informants. The experiences of teachers and students are included in the same chapter, as the expressions of this experience are enmeshed with each other. It is not always possible to separate the discussions of the experience or to discern where one begins and the other ends.

The teachers answered questions that began in a general way about their life and background; then they moved toward their philosophies of teaching and general attitudes about teaching. Next, they moved more specifically to questions concerning the development of relationships with students and the importance of these relationships. Finally, teachers answered questions asked about the challenges they faced in school with regard to developing relationships. The principal and staff members answered questions about their backgrounds, their educational philosophies, and their roles in the school. The students were asked about their families and backgrounds, their favorite teachers, and what they liked about these teachers. These questions, listed in the appendices, give us a sense of the participants' experiences and are analyzed through the ethic of care.

This research uses these individuals to describe a somewhat positive school environment, which we can call caring. Many of the students and teachers at the Newcomer Academy described their experiences, or the way they were treated, as being like a family. For the most part, the students' needs were met, and the adults discussed their roles at the school as positive and rewarding. The characterizations and anecdotes that follow are not models or descriptions of the way things should be. Tolstoy's *Anna Karenina*, tells a story of an unhappy family. The opening quotation of the novel sums up the basis of the main issue of the story that unfolds: "All happy families are alike; each unhappy family is unhappy in its own way" (2000, p. 1) From the opening line in Tolstoy's *Anna Karenina*, first published in 1887, we see that happy family interactions can have a common and universal experience. However, the stories of unhappy families begin to show fragmentation and must be detailed to describe the numerous ways in which the process can be derailed. These stories focus on the positive experiences as a way to show their importance for both teachers and students.

## Interpreting Data through the Ethic of Care

Four teachers and their teams, the principal, and three support staff at the Newcomer Academy were interviewed with guiding questions that were shaped by concerns and issues of the care theory. As part of the process of collecting anecdotes about the classroom experience, the individual informants defined or articulated many of the key concepts that Noddings described theoretically in her work (2003). The guiding questions, which were developed to capture different aspects of the caring experience, delineate and document the actual practice of care from the experiences in the classroom. These descriptions operationalize care or give specific details of how the care theory is used in practice from the description of the experience of care.

## The Ethic of Care

Noddings developed the care ethic or theory over a number of years (1984, 1995, 2002, 2003). Care theory involves three main areas of caring: caring about learning (aesthetic caring); taking a caring stance as a professional position, regardless of a lack of response from the student or cared-for (ethical caring); and relational caring, the kind of care or attention that is memorable to both students and teachers, as we will see in the following presentation. Further, this aspect of relational care holds true for studies that involve Latino populations (Valenzuela, 1999) and African American students (Polite & Davis, 1999). This chapter and the next are concerned primarily with the relational aspect of care.

## Aesthetic Caring (Caring about Learning)

Aesthetic caring is a regard for an intellectual act or knowing. In schools, this knowledge is regarded as the supreme concern because students go to school to learn, and teachers, it is usually universally agreed, go to school to teach. In their discussions, the teachers spoke of the importance of their subject matter. Jesse, the math teacher made it very clear why students and teachers were there:

> Learning is what they are here for. I mean, they don't get up at 5 o'clock in the morning and try to make it out here because they are forced to do this; it's because they want to. They want to learn. I say, "I am here to teach you, and for you guys to learn."

## Preparing the Stage

Before students can learn, teachers must create a stage or place for learning. When we enter the room of the art teacher, we immediately see that it's different from other rooms in the school. Artwork covers every available space and includes pieces of art from each student. One such exhibit is the wall of faces that stare out at us, one face representing each student. When placed side by side, one atop another, row after row, the faces create an impression of a community in which individuals fit into a greater design. Each one is unique, but all are united. This wall alone creates a sense of belonging in the art classroom. The fluorescent lights in the room are turned off; instead, lamps around the room provide the light to create a mood of creativity and otherworldliness. Soft music plays as we enter and breathe in the ambience. This is a school, right? Well, it's the art room, and the mood and stage are set for what is to take place there. Jennifer, the art teacher, explains:

> The students feel comfortable when they come in here because they know I care for them...and that I'm doing everything I can for them...I make this like a mini-home, too. I think the students feel good in here. It's a safe place...they get to socialize a little, and they get to be creative and use the side of the brain that they don't get to use most of the day.

The science teacher created another kind of space, but nonetheless, she set the stage for learning in her classroom. When we pop in there, we see students walking about in the purposeful pursuit of paper, markers, scales, or other items. They may even be looking for people—anything or anyone needed for their laboratory work. One aspect of science class is that the students work at tables in groups. Students at each table are involved in different activities and engaged at various stages. Some students are standing and pointing for the others to see. One student talks with the teacher as if they are peers; both are scientists involved in the pursuit of answers to questions of mutual interest. The students move easily, and indeed, this school does not seem like others, where deadly order prevails when we enter the room.

Eduardo, a student from Cuba, talked about a classroom that invited him to study because of its homelike feeling:

> She had a couch area. You could walk anywhere you wanted, and wherever you felt the most pleasant—the tables, couch, on the floor, wherever you wanted. You find where you are comfortable; it's not like you have to be at a desk.

No matter what form the classroom took,whether to set a mood, as in the art room; or to create a laboratory experience, as in the science room; or students working in pairs on problems for the math class, each teacher created an environment where learning can take place.

## Love of Learning

Teachers worked to make learning something students could love. Jesse reiterated the students' interest in learning and the teachers' interest in helping the students learn.

> If they needed me to stay after school, or they needed me to come whenever they wanted to, I would help them out as much as possible, especially if they were doing what they were supposed to be doing.

Melissa, the English teacher, explained that she did not give students homework unless they needed extra work or did not do the work in class:

> For some kids who just blew off the assignment that day, I will say, "That is your homework." I have done things for students who needed more: "Do this tonight." But they travel so far... they are on the bus for an hour and a half. They don't get home until 7 o'clock.

Jon, a student from Pakistan, talked about how thankful he and other students were that his math teacher at the neighborhood school stayed late and tutored after school. Jon, who was now in his senior year, described his teacher:

> She teaches pre-calculus and they (the students) need help. She is there from 8 o'clock in the morning to 8 o'clock in the evening... Sometimes, when I need help, I go there.

When asked why they were at school, the students would instinctively tell anyone, "To learn." They may have also been there because their friends were at school, because it was a habit, or because it was better than staying at home (all of these were responses I received as to why a student goes to school). Both students and teachers knew that school was for learning.

## Ethical Caring (Caring Even When a Student Doesn't Respond)

We might ask, then, why it's necessary for teachers to take an ethical stance. We could ask why a teacher would not like some students, or why students would act as though they did not want to study or know what is being discussed. We might wonder why students are sent to the office for being disruptive. We could question why teachers must act as though they care, and why students act as though they don't. Caring is a stance or a role that can be modeled in order to help the moral development of the student. Educators will act as though they care so that students will think that someone cares for them and will want to learn.

I asked teachers how they dealt with students who were disruptive or needed extra attention. Teachers gave various answers to explain how they worked with these students. Rocio, the social worker said:

> We've got to find the strengths...We have to find out what that student's strengths are. Everybody has strengths, even though sometimes it's hard to see them because they are buried so far underneath...

An interesting comment came from Ana, the school registrar who sometimes monitored the students when they served a time out or detention:

> I had one student who came to me and was very loud and disruptive when he was put in time out. His weakness was that he did not like to be ignored, so when I found that this bothered him, then I ignored him. When I didn't acknowledge him, then he would seek me out because I had ignored him. Then I would acknowledge him because he came to me without his loud, "Look at me! Look at me!" For me, it is finding a weakness.

The way Bill, the history teacher, handled a situation would most likely depend on the student:

> It depends on the problem. Some students are attention-hungry—negative or positive, they don't care. So, we have to be able to hone that desire for attention. They want someone to pay attention to them and talk to them. We've got to do it, but not at the expense of the content or the pace of the class.

Eduardo, a student from Cuba who graduated, attended a nearby university and returned to mentor students. He shared an insight into the situation:

> I notice the ones that are distracting or disrupting the class. I know exactly what to do with them. I have to say that I don't like them...they make me think of myself, and nobody likes to see himself like that!

Even the students knew when they had crossed a line. If a teacher did not call them on their transgression, then the students would wonder why. However, adolescent life moves fast, and students will not wonder for long; instead, they will continue to stay on the other side of the line or the law if no one points out where the line is. Eduardo went on to say that often the students who misbehaved were smart and just bored. Jesse, the math teacher, was formerly one such student, which is why he kept his classes challenging and knew when the students started trying to con him for a way to get out of class.

## Relational Caring

Although students and teachers alike acknowledged that schools are places set up for learning, it does not take long to realize or understand that the way teachers approach the students and the way students respond to teachers are big parts of the learning process. When talking about any topic related to school, learning, or students, the nature of the relationships between the teachers and students, or the importance and need to understand what the student is like or what the students like, begin to dominate the conversation. Even when talking about an appreciation of knowledge or discussing aesthetic or ethical care, these discussions will begin to edge toward the way the interactions take place between the teacher (the one caring) and the student (the one cared for) and the nuances that affect the transfer of information within this relationship. Relational caring refers to reciprocity, or a mutual feeling, that is felt and develops in a caring relationship between at least two people. This research discusses the relationship between an educator and a student. Relational caring can also correspond to relationships that develop between peers (teachers), or between the administration and the staff. In this study, regardless of who is involved in the relationship, I will describe circumstances that form relational situations for the purpose of learning.

The relational aspect is emphasized and complements the aesthetic care, which values knowledge and the acquisition of information. "A student will care about what you say, when you care about the student" (Sergiovanni, 2006). Placing a value on information is one kind of caring, but in the care literature, the emphasis is placed on both the relational aspect of the ethic of care and the moral development of the cared-for from this relationship.

As Jesse, the math teacher, repeated over and over, "They will care about math because they care about the teacher." Denise, the science teacher, said, "Absolutely, they learn through the relationship." Melissa, the English teacher, talked about how important the band director in her high school was for her survival as a teenager because of the instability in her home. Jennifer, the art teacher, related that she didn't feel normal until she met her art teachers:

> Well, I always admired my art teachers—my middle school and high school art teachers. They were my reason to go to class. They had different perspectives. I really liked that it is okay to be different; and it's okay to express myself; and just that everything is not on this straight path. I have choices. They opened doors for me.

We can use the teachers' descriptions of themselves as students to help articulate the importance of the relationship. It may not be until the students who were interviewed for this study get older that they themselves can describe the importance of that relationship; so to some extent, I have relied on the teachers' experiences as students to put that aspect of the relationship into words.

Students agreed that they were going to want to pay attention if they liked the teacher. It is not necessary to like the teacher, but it certainly seems to help. The relationship also affects the way that information is conveyed through interviews. When I observed a class, students may have minimized the importance of what they said to me or answered politely because I am an adult and a former teacher. However, it was clear when students felt comfortable in a classroom setting: Their body language and their focus on the lesson showed that they were interested—regardless of what they said or did not say to me in an interview.

One reason that this immigrant population especially needs to have caring teachers is that they have often left family members in their home country, or relatives in another country or city. These students are newly transplanted in a country with new relatives, or part of a family they may not be close to, and in a culture that is not always as warm to them as they were accustomed to in their home. One of their unrecognized needs is to understand the institution's processes and the mechanisms of the school (Stanton-Salazar, 1997).

## Relational Caring: The One Caring

In the teacher-student relationship, the teacher or adult has been referred to as the one caring, and the student as the cared-for (Noddings, 1984, 2003). Each of the four teachers who were interviewed discussed the importance of caring for students; that is, the relational aspects of caring. Each teacher gave a definition of what it meant to care. For Jennifer, the art teacher, the definition meant standing by what you say you will do:

> You define care with the little things you do. If you say you are going to do something, you do it; you don't back off or give an excuse because if they see that you back off, then they can do the same thing.

Jennifer said caring for the students also means thinking about the students beyond the classroom:

> When I go home, I am thinking about them and what we are going to do the next day, or of a conversation that we had. An example of something silly: I brought lotion for after the clay projects because their hands feel awful after we do clay. And so, anyone who wants lotion, they come up and get in line and I squeeze little drops.

Further, caring considers the constraints that the students' lives impose on them, such as their long bus rides and the responsibilities that they have for their families. It doesn't mean that the teacher will let students do anything they want to do, though. Jennifer expected students to behave respectfully.

> It takes them a long time to get here every day, so I want to be here for them. The students are usually well behaved, but last week some boys were acting out, making orgasmic noises, and I sent them to the principal. Word spread pretty fast, "That is not cool in her class...she gets pretty mad at that stuff."

Jesse the math teacher mirrored the art teacher's definition:

> How would I define care? I feel for these kids, as I would for a family member, as if they were my cousins.

However, Jesse talked about what happened when students tried to take advantage of him:

> At the end of the last six weeks, some kids came up to me and asked for help. "Well, I don't see how you expect me to help you right now, when you didn't do anything in class. I'm not going to waste my time, if you didn't want to listen to me and do anything in class."

Again, he would do anything he could for these students, but it did not mean that he would let them take advantage of him, or that he would accept everything that was done. The relationship was a two-way street, and he made sure the students understood that condition. Over and over again in his comments, he pointed out how he explained the processes of school to his students. He talked them through the process of understanding consequences, as he did above. Other comments he made further illustrated this point.

Denise, a science teacher, extended the discussion about care by calling it a form of love:

> No, I think it actually is showing love. Now, I wouldn't want to actually say that, because it has got such a negative social connotation, even though that sounds crazy. I would never say, "I love you," but instead, "I care about you," and "You are my student, and I really care about you. I respect you, and I cherish you." That would probably be about as far as I would go. I probably wouldn't ever say the word love, but at the very end, when they are graduating, leaving us and moving on, I have had students tell me, "I love you so much." And then, of course, I will say, "I love you so much, too." When they bring it up, I would not feel uncomfortable to talk about it. But I don't want to make them feel uncomfortable and get the wrong idea about anything, either.

Denise showed me how this love extends into the classroom and affects the way a teacher approaches the subject matter. One day, as I walked down the hall, she ran to catch me. She told me that she had an experience that made her think of how caring about students' feelings shows up in the classroom. She wanted to share it with me. Her act of finding me to say that she had been thinking about our conversations was a caring act in itself. She commented on how she and another science teacher adjusted an activity to consider how a student would feel:

> Today we were planning a warm-up activity. Another teacher was planning an activity that involved measuring the smallest and biggest body parts of students: feet, hands, tallest, shortest, and so on. Well, as the student who was always tallest and had the biggest feet, I immediately knew that it could cause discomfort with students, so I suggested that we measure inanimate objects to get the idea of measurement across without affecting any students' feelings...

This is an example of how care can look in a classroom. The English teacher, Melissa, talked about care in her class with her students:

> If they don't care, they are not going to want to learn it or think it is important for them to learn it. And most of the connecting I have done has been on that emotional base of showing them I care.

When asked if she feels like they go along with her because they like her, she said, "I think so. I think that is what it is riding on."

Caring is central to the learning process. It seems hard to separate it from the learning. We will see this relationship repeatedly in the examples that both the teachers and students gave. Students did not talk at such length, but each of them had an opinion about what it is to be cared for and its importance.

## Relational Caring: The One Cared-for

The student is the one who feels the relationship. The student or child is said to glow or grow when involved in this kind of relationship with an adult. Reciprocity and relation are two terms used in the discussions of this relationship. Without responsiveness or a response on the part of the cared-for, we cannot say that a caring relationship exists. The reciprocity that exists between the two people is what confirms the relationship. A sense of joy can also be said to be a part of the care process (Noddings, 1984, 1996, 2003). Students involved in a caring relationship will have an expression on their faces that is missing from students who do not know that feeling.

Martine, a student, said that what made a favorite teacher was the way the teacher talked to him—the way the teacher presented the information and asked if he needed help, individually. "But sometimes the teacher doesn't know how to explain the information, or the students didn't understand the first time," he said. Another student, Robbie, a Cuban, mentioned how he liked his coaches and one coach in particular because of the way he approached the students. In addition to the individual explanations, the way the teacher talks with the student seems to really matter. This point came up time and time again in conversations with students: "They talk with us like a friend," or "She worries about us," or "She's fun."

At a large school, the overall effect may not be felt if only one teacher here and one teacher there practices care. At the Newcomer Academy, many of the students demonstrated that they cared, which, along with the tone set by the principal and support staff, created an especially caring culture at the school. During a conversation with the three Cuban students in their junior year at the neighborhood school, I asked them who had been their favorite teacher at the Newcomer Academy. "Any of them," they answered. They missed all of the teachers. They missed the school because, as a whole, they felt that the teachers understood them and made it feel like a home. They had fond memories of their experiences there. This is the experience of care.

*Why do they not tell
what they know?
Why can't they relate to the
young ones, wanting,
the young ones, so earnestly seeking*

—Barbara McKinley, *Second Verse* (2006, p. 64)

# 5

## Practice of Care

### Building Relationships

*The difficulty lies not so much in developing new ideas
as in escaping from old ones.*

—Ken Blanchard (2010, p. 227)

## Relational Caring: Initiating Relationships: Conveying Availability to the Student

Many teachers wait for students to ask for help, but for students to feel comfortable in doing so, they must have had positive experiences with adults or teachers. Martine said, "My grandmother told me to respect adults and be humble. She told me to listen and be around the right people." Although these traits are passive, I asked him whether his relationship with his grandmother was the reason he felt comfortable asking teachers for help; he answered, "Yes." Even though he had been instructed to listen, be respectful, and be humble—all traits that a teacher can appreciate—it was because he was close to his grandmother that he felt safe enough to say to a science teacher, "We don't understand you. Can you please explain more simply?" For Martine, this one conversation with his teacher had been enough. I don't know how much it really helped the rest of the class, but because Martine had taken the initiative, he was satisfied in that class.

Teachers and students alike had mixed responses about who should initiate their relationship. One thing that seems certain is that most students need it; if students don't initiate it, then teachers need to. Alicia felt that she should initiate the relationship but only did so with one or two teachers. She didn't feel comfortable asking an attendance clerk about absences and didn't know whom to talk with to find out about the processes for getting help with a problem outside of school. She felt awkward in asking for any kind of help from an adult she didn't already know. Apparently, no teachers had initiated relationships with her, or she didn't feel comfortable asking a teacher at Lee High School about her personal problems.

Olivia, on the other hand, felt that it was up to her to do well and to ask for help. A teacher, even her favorite teacher, would have a number of students she saw on any given day, which made it hard for her to help Olivia individually. Olivia mentioned a math teacher who made her feel comfortable within the past year when she invited her to eat lunch during her free time. The math teacher helped students individually and made them feel comfortable. Olivia reported that the following year, the same teacher taught statistics, but she apparently did not feel at ease with the topic. Because of her discomfort, the math teacher seemed like a totally different person. In class, she would ask if students understood. When the two *good* students in class said "Yes," the math teacher moved on to the next topic.

Olivia was struck by how different the teacher was this year in the more difficult class. Olivia mentioned that teachers needed to be closer to their students, but her responses were contradictory when I asked if teachers should help students with personal problems. High school students want teachers to be open to them. The students want the teachers to be approachable and take the initiative by circulating in class and asking them individually if they understand, but not to pry into individual matters or go too far with the relationship. If a student does need extra help, then asking the teachers for it will be a comfortable and natural process if the teachers make their availability apparent. Students want help on academic matters, but on personal matters, only in a selective way and only with certain adults.

One way that Melissa, the English teacher, conveyed her availability was to eat lunch with students in the cafeteria.

There will be one or two days I won't go, but I like to go down to the cafeteria. What I did at first was, I would sit with kids whom no one was sitting with, or maybe someone I felt needed a presence there. Later, I started sitting at a table by myself. It's really funny. Now, this one group of boys sits next to me. We talk in English as much as we can. Sometimes, it goes into Spanish, but we try to have conversations in English.

Amber, a student from Mexico who has returned to Stafford High School after two years at the Newcomer Academy, said:

The students need to put school first. They have to like the school. I don't like the school (Stafford), but I like some of the teachers. Teachers need to have a lot of activities and things so that the students can understand in class. Teachers can be strict and still be like a friend.

Jon, a Pakistani student who often had to maneuver school alone, was very bright and definitely put school first. He said he was usually comfortable in class, but "It is easier if a teacher pays attention to you and makes you feel comfortable." Martha said that teachers always encouraged her and asked her if she needed help. Teachers came to her, perhaps because they saw that she worked so hard.

Raul, a student from Mexico, resented a teacher who treated him like a small child.

I think that teachers discourage students when they treat a kid just as if he was too much of a troublemaker or something like that. I got treated like that once by one of my teachers, just because I used to talk in class (which everyone did). I was only in class for the first five minutes when this teacher sent me outside to wait to have a talk. But like always, this teacher would leave me outside, waiting the entire class period.

Teachers said that to have relationships with students, they merely gave instructions, put the students to work, and then circulated in order to work with students individually. Jennifer, the art teacher, said:

I start the relationships by just sitting down with them. I think they start feeling comfortable when I am at the tables, doing my work; and they are doing their work. And sometimes, we don't even talk. We're just sitting next to each other.

Denise, the science teacher, showed her availability by giving her students information about her own life. It was an easy way to start the relationship and signal that she, as a teacher, regarded the students as people first.

Maybe, just have an interest in them, and also a willingness to share some details of my life; not a lot of details, but something about the pictures of my children—these are their names. And there are inevitably questions about that, so I answer those and just tell them a little bit more: "And they are just like you; they are the same age as you. They are two years older," or whatever, compared to them, things like that.

Another way that Denise initiated relationships was to play card games with the students in the cafeteria: "Playing games is a really good way, especially when you don't speak the language, to become included. A real simple card game works very well." Peers, administrators, and students selected the teachers who were interviewed at the Newcomer Academy as caring teachers, so it makes sense that the students felt comfortable opening up to these teachers about personal matters. Some of the students said that any of the Newcomer Academy teachers were caring; if this statement was true, then it would be an added reason why the students felt comfortable in the school.

## Relational Caring: Responsiveness, Reciprocity, and Confirmation

Whether the teacher or the student starts the relationship is hard to say. But what does seem to be described in the process is that one responds, and the other reciprocates or confirms. The student, or one cared-for, feels confirmed. The teacher is responsive. A reciprocal relationship and process are taking place. In other words, it is hard to know which one confirms and which one feels the confirmation, or which one responds and which one reciprocates. What we can say is that often in a classroom, if students do not feel a warmth or bond, they will say things such as, "The class feels boring," "The teacher doesn't explain," "He's too busy," "He sits at his computer," or some other indication that the students do not feel important to the teacher. Plato, in the *Phaedrus* (1995), explained that it is hard to tell who is the one loving and who the beloved is. Because responsiveness and confirmation feel the same, it is hard to know who initiates this reciprocal process. It may seem that the student is the beloved, but in fact, Socrates indicated in *Phaedrus* that the student's hunger brings out the teacher. What is not clear is what sparks that hunger in the student, and why sometimes the teacher lacks the interest or ability to respond.

Students talked about a favorite teacher, liking a class, or going to the Newcomer Academy office every day. However, it was hard for them to describe the relationship in detail or explain the specific aspects. Students sometimes showed their appreciation by giving the teacher gifts. Denise said:

Well, I have gotten many beautiful pictures that they have drawn for me; beautiful pictures, colored, sometimes inscribed very beautifully and sometimes not so beautifully. But the sentiment is there. I have gotten some poems. I have gotten little gifts and trinkets, and lots of hugs.

When I was a teacher, the walls of my classroom were covered with artwork from the students. These expressions, as well as the offers to brush my hair during lunch, could be taken as a sign of reciprocation, or initiation. The girls always wanted to make me over. I often felt that those sessions with the lunch girls were as much for me as for the students. During those times, I was able to understand a great deal about the students by getting to know them outside of class, and we shared moments that were not always available during class time. Students shared wedding photos, told me about boyfriends, and asked me for direction in their life. Generally, though, we had fun together.

Teachers seem much freer to talk about experiences with their students and, perhaps, about their experiences with memorable teachers of their own. Melissa, a new teacher, stated: "I haven't taught long enough. Probably, when I've taught for a few years and students come back, then I'll know if it was transformative or important for them." More likely than not, teachers do not hear back from their students. Sometimes, we run into students at a store or somewhere in the community, or we hear of stories by chance. Students wanted to be helpful and responsive when I asked them questions, but the depth of the relationship often was not conveyed in their answers so much as by the fact that they took time and care to answer questions at all. Further, the students may not have the maturity to see the importance until a later date or may need more time for reflection, which is all a part of the subtlety of the relationship.

Jesse, the math teacher, talked about how his students got so excited that they wanted to teach others about what they had just learned. "Oh, ahh!" and "Wow!" sprinkled his conversations about the students' enthusiasm to learn math and connect it to what they had learned earlier. Jesse and his mentor, another math teacher, also spoke of how students would bring in problems for them (the teachers) to solve while the students did their daily warm-ups in class.

I was explaining to them that multiplying a polynomial is the same thing as looking for the area of a rectangle or a square. The way most teachers teach it is confusing; it is really hard to see. So I showed them how to do the area, and they said, "Wow!" It's the exact same thing, I told them. It's good for these kids because they need to be able to *see* what's going on in math.

Another reason that students experienced "ah-ha!" moments with Jesse is that, as a Hispanic who grew up in the border area, he mirrored to the students a more grown-up version of themselves. "They are like, 'Wow, I can't do anything because this guy knows my next step; he has been there.' So it kind of makes a pretty good relationship between us."

Jennifer said that her art teacher was the only one who understood her and helped her feel normal:

> My middle school art teacher let me know there were choices. My teacher gave me a reason to go to school. She let me know that it's okay to be different, to express yourself. The art teachers also helped because they let me operate out of my artistic side. I did things a different way. My teacher was laid back. Deadlines were not written in stone. We worked outside a lot. We walked around together, often with cameras. I didn't do well with structure; the art teachers didn't give us a straight-up syllabus. I couldn't "stay in this line here." I was in tune with emotions and circumstances outside of the classroom.

Anabel, as the principal, set the tone for the school and allowed her teachers to feel safe and protected. She showed her teachers that she understood their needs. The art teacher told the principal, "If you leave, I'm quitting." Anabel was mentoring Jesse, the math teacher, to become a principal. The science teacher said repeatedly that the principal set the tone. One time, when Anabel overcorrected a student, the faculty spoke at great length about how she had gone to the student's house to apologize to him and his parent.

"This is why we have a caring environment here," said Denise, a science teacher. "When the principal showed that she could apologize to a student, we, as a faculty, were very touched by that."

The principal's own description of a high school teacher who had a big influence on her epitomized the tone she strove to set:

> He brought everything to us in the class. We went to so many places and saw so many things, all in his lessons. Sometimes he would come in dressed as the guy from—Harrison Ford, you know, in *The Raiders of the Lost Ark*. Well, that was before Harrison Ford. I mean, he would just come in with a big whip. And the lesson was thematic about whatever it was that he was teaching, but he would get into character. He had classical music going on at the beginning of class; we would come in, and the warm-up was to put into words the music you were hearing. Then, you had to name it. It was Beethoven's this or that or the other. You had to try to describe it as if a per-

son was deaf and couldn't hear the music, but they were reading your words; could they hear the music in your words?

All of that was just very powerful for me when I was in high school. He covered the wall with paintings, like Picasso—all the periods. Then, we got into the literature that was related to the periods of Picasso's moods, and he asked, "What was Picasso's thinking when he did this, and when he put this together? Now, let's read a story that has to do with, you know, the Blue Period." He connected all these things and just kind of opened our minds and our eyes. I can tell you that a day doesn't go by that I don't use something that he taught me in that class.

He was not a strict disciplinarian because the students, in wanting to be enthralled, made the others be quiet so that the mood would not be spoiled:

> You knew what you could and couldn't do in there. He had a very subtle way of bringing order to the moment. There was never disorder in his class, and there was a procedure, but I don't think of the teacher as strict. You had to behave in order to be a part of the class. You wanted to behave in a way that he expected, because it would be awful if he had to stop teaching to deal with behavior. The peer pressure—everyone wanted you to just close your mouth because he was saying something. It was just great—yes—magic!

She still wrote to that teacher from time to time because she felt, even after all of these years, she had not conveyed to him how important he was in her life. She did not care if he wrote back. For her to be able to express it was enough—and what mattered.

> He has never responded. I don't care. I used to see [his writings in magazines]. I don't care if he ever responds; I feel it's my duty to let him know how powerful he was in shaping me. Sometimes, teachers don't know what they do day after day.

The confirmation for the teacher was Anabel's letters that came every once in a while. For Anabel, the confirmation came during the class time, when the teacher opened up new worlds to her. It confirmed a new way of seeing things, and that was the hook for her.

Sometimes confirmation may come in a different way. Both Denise and Melissa talked about having crushes on their teachers. I asked Margaret why she decided to be a biology teacher:

> Well, I was in love with my high school biology teacher, but that was a separate issue. Oh, he was so handsome and young; yes, he was handsome. And we had a nickname for him since he was a biology teacher: Dr. Reproduc-

tion. He had live animals; I think he was pretty good. I seem to have learned some things.

Responsiveness, reciprocity, and confirmation take many forms and appearances. In reality, these confusions can exist, especially if there is a need in a student's life for confirmation that is not being met in the home. Alternately, a balanced student can acknowledge the confusion but not act on it, as in both Melissa and Denise's case. For the most part, we work past the ambiguity by sending nonverbal cues and keeping the attention on the schoolwork. I once asked the students, "How do you know a teacher cares for you?" A Vietnamese student, Kim, answered, "It is through the eyes." There is a great deal of eye contact at the Newcomer Academy, and a great deal is communicated that cannot really be discussed. Bob Dylan's words come to mind: "To look in a teacher's face complete." With the immigrant students, much freer and purer exchanges can take place through the eyes. It is difficult to analyze this phenomenon or try to discuss it with any integrity or honesty in an academic paper; I would probably have to use poetry or fictionalize the accounts. The emotional exchange is that strong. As Margaret, the science teacher, said, "I won't use the word love when referring to caring about the students, but it is that. If they come back to visit me, or on the last day, if they say, 'I love you,' then I will say, 'I love you, too.' They need to say it first."

As easily as Melissa had brought up the subject of crushes and teachers, she let it go, just as easily as Margaret did with her high school teacher. Both teachers found it simple enough to understand, dismiss, and move on from this topic. Melissa did talk at length about her high school band teacher and their everyday conversations after school. Because she acted out in school, she would get mixed messages of another kind from a number of her teachers, for instance, from her science teacher:

> There were letters home to my parents. I remember seeing this letter that my science teacher wrote, which said all these good things about me. I didn't feel that she felt those things at school. It was always, "Melissa, you need to stop. Melissa," you know, always harping on me; and then, seeing this letter that said, "Melissa is very intelligent," and "We need to work with her" was a big surprise to me. Seeing this note affected me.

However, it was the band director who, in Melissa's words, "saved me from this life of staying in the boonies."

> He was just awesome. I mean, it was one of those things where it was totally a relationship thing . . . I look back, and I say, "My band experience was about

the relationships, you know, between friends, between the band members, between me and my teacher."

Melissa explained that her mother often did not come to pick her up until 6:00 p.m. because she had to travel back from Houston every day. Her high school band teacher may have been the person who helped her make it through high school. Her home life was rocky with a stay-at-home, alcoholic, bipolar dad, and a mom who worked really long hours. Melissa had long conversations with the band director because he was there—and so was she.

Raul, a Mexican student, was one of the most articulate students in English at the Newcomer Academy. He was able to communicate why he liked his computer teacher: "He used to do so many things for students...he would teach us as much as he knew. He would make an entire class just for one student to learn, if this student really wanted to. He would even learn new stuff to teach us." Raul wanted to learn about computers, so the teacher told him to take a computer apart and put it back together. Raul did that and felt very proud. The teacher said, "Okay, do that again." Raul did it three more times.

> This teacher would be always in the classroom for anyone who would want to go and learn. He used to not just talk with students about schoolwork or things like that; he would even help with problems a student had outside school. If a student needed to get a job, he would go and talk to a CIS group to get help for this student. This teacher did not care whether you were white, black, green, red, or whatever color. This teacher would help you if you really cared about learning. He was not all about work or homework, or things like that. He was about learning, fun, and being interesting. He would keep his class as fun as possible to get students interested in it.

Memories of teachers like this one linger and can last a lifetime. Alicia wrote about what it was like to meet her father for the first time when she was 15 years old. For the first time in her life, she had someone who believed in her. A teacher can have the same profound effect on students. Olivia talked about her English teacher, who taught her how to speak English: "When I first came, all I knew how to say were the colors. Dr. Andradi took extra time with me."

Interestingly, when I spoke with Olivia two years later, she hardly remembered having told me that. She barely mentioned him. He taught her English, but she felt he had too many students to really get to know her. It will be interesting to see what she says in five years. Another intriguing note is that, as a teacher, I had a profound experience in learning about the students' culture. They wrote a play together during the advisory period. I learned about *Día de los Muertos*, and in the process of working on the play with the students, I felt close to them. The students may not have felt the same way. When I ran into some of these advisory students in the library, I asked them about the play and wanted them to talk about it. They had already forgotten about it, just like Olivia had forgotten the teacher who had taught her English. They laughed a lot about that discrepancy. Apparently, writing the play had only been important to me but was only a passing moment to them. Perhaps the most striking thing about that incident was that I could speak with these students about it, and we could laugh together about my misunderstanding—and my own need for it to be important. What students will carry with them is unpredictable.

It may be hard to say how the relationship between a student and a teacher begins. In each of my classes, one or two students would come forward after class and start asking questions, or they asked if they could stay in at lunch.

One student in particular would ask questions and tell me things. In a way, this student began to act as a medium or go-between, explaining the other students to me. Celia Mendoza was her name. She would say things such as, "Please, Miss, we need to learn English. We need you to explain this." In time, if I ever had a question or doubt about something, I would ask Celia. She and a group of girls came in every day at lunch to use the computers, and they helped each other navigate that first year of school together. Perhaps I conveyed availability, and she responded or reciprocated. The confirmation came in the way we greeted each other, the way we passed time together daily in agreeable ways, and in the way that we grew to count on each other. It may be that Celia was more mature than the other students and was able to feel comfortable initiating a relationship. In so doing, she taught me how to relate to the other students.

In contrast, a student can initiate the relationship in another way; he or she may act out. One boy, Galileo, was always trying to mess up the class. He had a need for the class to stop what it was doing and look at him. Ms. Terry, the teaching assistant, and I helped him by giving him attention before he asked for it. I started going to his soccer games, and that almost transformed him overnight. One time when I didn't go, he asked, "Where were you?" It is amazing how a gesture from a teacher can become important, especially if a student has a special need.

The one caring, the one cared-for; the one showing availability, the one responding; all of these distinctions become quickly confused and intertwined in a school environment where people see each other every day in close proximity. That give-and-take creates the family or community feeling in a school.

## Relational Caring: Engrossed/Engaged

When teachers talked about their enthusiasm for their classes, I felt that their words showed an engrossment in their work and with their students. Several teachers and staff members, in the course of speaking of something else, said spontaneously, "I love my job" as a way of trying to put into words what they were trying to convey. Jennifer, the art teacher, said, "I love my job. Sometimes I would rather say I am an art teacher than, like, a wife." Mr. Monster, the computer technician echoed the same sentiment with statements such as:

> I love my job... Interacting with the students is not difficult for me. I have fun. I like to have fun with the students. I like to let them know that they are at home here, and that they are comfortable with being here. So, when we talk, it is usually different than being their teacher. They can come to me and talk to me, or we can have fun. I do things for students, like I fix computers on my own time for them. I assist them with homework; I don't actually do it for them. Just, if they have questions, you know, I help them in that way.

Jesse, the math teacher, went even further in describing his engrossment with the students:

> I don't give up, even if the kid tries to act up... I will still be nice to him in front of the class, and he won't always understand why. He'll ask, "Why are you doing that?" I will say, "Because I care about you." I would tell him, in front of the class, "I love you!" He'll say, "What?" And the student says, "Ah, you are gay!" And I say, "No, I am not gay... I really want you pass this class." I say, "I know that if I ask you a question, you're going to give me the correct answer." And I ask him something that he knows the answer to, and when he answers, I'll say, "There you go. See? You have been paying attention and just pretending. I know you are."

When the teachers were engrossed, the students were engaged. It meant a lot to Raul, the student from Mexico, that a teacher would do extra things for them outside of class.

> This teacher would help you if you really cared about learning. This teacher was not all about work or homework or things like that. He was about learning, fun, and being interesting.

Another student, Leticia, an El Salvadorian student, commented about her math teacher, "If you don't understand, she spends more time with you." Martha, an Ethiopian student, talked about her favorite teacher: "My accounting teacher talks about her personal life. She talks about her past and what she did. I like that."

A Cuban student, Eduardo, said that in his native country, the teachers and students were friends: "We went to parties together all the time. On Fridays, when they got their paychecks, we were together all the time."

> *We meet at the edge of pain*
> *Not to stay there, but to find our way home . . .*
>
> —Barbara McKinley, *Second Verse* (2006, p. 38)

# 6

## The Practice of Care

### A Transformational Aspect

*We are such stuff*
*as dreams are made on . . .*
—William Shakespeare (*The Tempest*)

## Relational Caring: Attunement with Students

Engrossed teachers also imply a kind of attunement to the needs of the students, in this case, their social, emotional, cultural, academic, and linguistic needs. Melissa summed up the ways in which she was attuned with the students from her own experiences with transnationalism and moving.

> Certainly, I felt very strong empathy with them because they didn't speak the language, and they were new and afraid. As you know, our students have a lot of other issues, too, like interrupted education and those kinds of things.

Denise also shared her strategy:

*Care & Advocacy: Narratives from a School for Immigrant Youth,* pages 65–78
Copyright © 2012 by Information Age Publishing
All rights of reproduction in any form reserved.

I took time to stop and spend some time with each one, learning their names; talking to them as best I could, even if I didn't speak their language.

Jennifer, the art teacher, was especially attuned to the students socially and helped them get to know other new students.

Well, there are some kids that will place themselves on the outside of groups. So, if I see that I can push them a little bit to open up, I will be like, "Hey, why don't you come sit over here?" You know, as a way of helping (them meet) each other, too. I help them move.

Jennifer had a heightened sensitivity because as a student, she moved between different kinds of social groups and didn't like being labeled as one kind of student or another. Melissa, the English teacher, had a similar background, which she described in this way:

I would jump groups. I had friends in every group, or every clique. But for a while, I felt more accepted by the slacker/stoner kids because they were cool. Maybe it is because they were always drugged up and didn't care—but I learned the system. I said, "Okay, to beat the system, I need to start dressing in a different way," so I did. I started dressing like a preppie, but it was so hypocritical, or I felt like it was.

Melissa was sensitive to students' social needs because one or two teachers had typecast her and therefore, she was ostracized from the National Honor Society. She knew that students can be "trying things out," and she was more open to them because of her own experiences with discouraging or judgmental teachers. In this way, she was attuned to the students and their social needs:

I don't know everyone's story. And one thing that we want to do here is to have them tell their story. I don't know everyone's story, but they help me understand. (A student) that is bouncing off the walls and who always wants water and always has an excuse—it makes a difference in my approach for me to know he has had two or three different guardians in the past. I know of two since he has been here. I know that he is coming from a home life that is not stable. I can relate to that. I was almost the same way. I relate to and understand those kids better than my kids that are very silent.

Jennifer, the art teacher, realized that some students needed to be alone and not connect with the teacher: "Some kids just don't want to be friends with a teacher, and we have to accept that. You can't force them."

Jesse let students sit alone for a while if they were out of sorts or acted as though they were not interested. He would then return when it was safe.

> If they are mad, I let them resist and stay mad, but time will pass and it will get resolved. They will sit there, and they will throw a fit. I think, "As long as you don't do anything to wreck my class, then just sit there and be bad." Afterwards, another kid will ask me something, and I will say out loud, "You see? This is the way you do things." I use the example of the boy who is upset. I make sure that I circle back to him after that happens. I make sure that I use it as an example later.

Jesse used that student as an example for others, too. He told this story about an incident with one student:

> I am not a very harsh teacher. I used to skip school, so I wanted to go and ask him, you know, "What is up? Here is the work. Finish it. Fine." I mean, you will find out your consequences for skipping later. I went up to him, and I said, "Hey, where were you?" And he says, "Oh, I went to go eat, and I didn't want to go to your class. Your class is boring." And I was thinking, "My class is boring because you don't pay attention."
>
> (The student said), "Well, I already missed it. Too bad. We can't do anything about it."
>
> "Oh, I can't do anything about it? I was going to let you slide," I told him. "I was going to let you do the work. But in that case, let's see how much I can do about it." I took him down to the office. They took his keys away. They ended up keeping his car here for three days because nobody could come and pick it up, and the assistant principal was only going to release it to a parent that had a license. So, it took three days for him to pick up his car. After school, one of the students was like, "Go to Mr. DelaHuerta (Jesse). Mr. DelaHuerta is cool; he will help you." And he turned around and looked at me, and he was like, "Well, he is the teacher that turned me in." The students told him he was stupid.

Jesse did not have to correct the student because the other students stepped in and let him know how he had crossed a line. Jesse had other interesting insights and ways of relating to the students. He said that he understood them because he had gone through much of what they were experiencing. He grew up on the border, English was his second language, and he struggled with learning English all his life.

> When they see that I was in the same boat a certain amount of years ago that they are in, it kind of hits them in the heart. And they are like, "You know what? I can't trick this guy by saying, 'Oh, I can't do that,' because he has

already been there." It hits them hard. "I know what you are going to do. I know what you are going to say. I know what excuses you are going to bring up. I know exactly what happened." So they can't get away with it, and it stumps them. They are like, "Wow!"

Jesse turned this cultural knowledge into a way to motivate the students with their schoolwork and academic needs. He was attuned to the students' tendencies to live in the present. He worked to take those blinders away from the students so they could have a more future-oriented perspective. He told them:

> "If you work now, you'll make a lot of money, but if you study and go to college, it will be easier for you down the line." In order to get to a kid, you need to take that blind spot away from them; (you must look into the future) and have him look forward, and say, "Well, what do you see?" That gets kids' attention. "You know what? I will see you back here next year because you are going to fail this class. I am not going to pass you. I am not one of those teachers that goes, 'Oh, poor kid,'" you know. I was like, "I was a poor kid, too." I was like, "I went through the same thing you did, and there is no reason why you can't do it. I care about you. And I am not about to pass you. If I pass you, and then you get to college and you can't do anything, it might screw up your whole life."

Denise used her focus and interest in the subject matter to motivate students, which showed that she was attuned to their needs:

> For one thing, I motivate through an interest in the subject. And then, also, I love those positive strokes, like everybody else. If my boss says, "So-and-so, you are doing a good job at this," then I puff up and I keep on going a little further. Also, of course, I want to do a good job, and I want my students to be successful. And doing a good job means that my students master this material, and that they can do well on the tests, and they are prepared in every possible way that I can help them.

Not only did Denise equate motivation with academics, but she also connected a student's need for attention (social and emotional) to performance. She felt that if she addressed those needs, the students would perform better. She tied her performance to theirs.

Besides the social, emotional, and academic aspects of being attuned, some teachers showed that they were aware of students' needs for extra attention to their linguistic abilities. Melissa, the English teacher, echoed the need to meet the academic needs of the students:

Just meet their needs... Start from the ground, and then go up. Right now, I don't think we are meeting (the) needs of our beginner students. For intermediate students, yes, we are, because they are at this level already. Just bring those, the bottom kids, up to a level where the things that we are presenting to them will be helpful. Instead of doing sheltered instruction, maybe do a fast-paced language program.

The art teacher used art as a medium through which she and the students could express emotional content without the constraints of words: "Art is a universal language, a way to get in with students fast, where we can agree on a different level. With art, they work between languages." Jennifer tried to use art as the language or medium through which they could share emotions and expression. She also made adjustments with her language and instruction. She took advantage of art and its use for communication: "I talk slower; and it's not really a language. It is more visual. I can just tell when I look across the room and they are not getting it, at that point. I can just kind of draw a picture on the board." Even still, Jennifer felt that she could not connect with the students as deeply as she would have liked because of the language barriers and constraints: "Sometimes I feel like I can't go back to the deep level that I want to get from them on the art because of the language barrier. So I can't take them where I wanted them to go. So that's sometimes frustrating."

Jesse encouraged the students to get past the fear of the new language and keep working at the math problems: "They see words and they shut down. That is one of the barriers I try to get rid of: 'Don't shut down right away; I need you to look at it, and you *do* know what you need to do.'" He communicated past barriers in a student's culture. He could communicate with students with more than language:

> Another story is about a boy from Africa who likes to play rough. He teases a girl, and she says, "Be quiet," pushes him and then starts to cry. A Chinese student tells the student from Africa that the teacher had told him to not push or touch students. So Tommie, the African boy, says, "My bad," and he works it out. So the communication can also mean knowing the kids; being there where you can "grab" them—and this can go beyond language, with the help of the other students because you are in tune with them.

Through the relationships and caring that the teachers have established in their classroom, they have created environments for students to become engrossed in their work. Being attuned to the students emotionally and socially is a part of the process.

## Relational Caring: Trust and Empathy

Students develop trust when teachers show empathy and are attuned. All of the teachers revealed that by drawing from their own childhood experiences, they understood the students. The art teacher said that she gave her students the benefit of the doubt from the first day:

> I trust you from day one. You walk in, I trust you. The only thing you can do is make me not trust you. And the first minute that there is something off, we will have that talk. Trust is harder to earn than just to have.

The science teacher moved a good deal when she was young, including a bi-national relocation. She understood the issues with attending different school systems, and the need for a student to feel welcomed and at home.

> It was really an eye-opener, a shocking experience. For one thing, also, we changed educational systems. We went from the American educational system to a British system, so we actually went to a British school. We had that reality check, which took my siblings and me from the top of the class straight to the bottom of the class. With no caring aspects in that school, we had that issue. And then, of course, the language issue was difficult, because we lived in an apartment building with people that didn't speak English.
>
> The British school system, from what I learned after being thrust into it, is an amazingly wonderful system if you start out that way. When you get thrown into it, as I was in the seventh grade, it was shocking. I had 13 major subjects, including physics, Latin, English, Spanish, French, chemistry, algebra, and geometry—and I can't even remember what else. It was very, very rigorous.
>
> There was very little nurturing, but the discipline—it was still kind of old school, very old school, where you have to study and have no second chances. And one of the things that always stuck in my mind was our first report card. We didn't realize how cruel they could be, in that they gave us a ranking in every single subject. So, say you had 26 kids in your class. (Maybe I would be) 25 or 26 in physics; 26 in chemistry; 20–24 in English. It was very, very, very, very demeaning. It really was awful.

Denise and Jesse both taught very rigorous and demanding subjects: science and math. In both classes, students had to pass state-mandated tests. Both teachers showed a great deal of understanding about the students from first-hand experience, and both pushed the students in their classes, using the same textbooks as the rest of the schools in the district. Margaret said, "We won't read as much, but we cover the same material." Jesse said the same thing about math: "This is one of the subjects that is taught the same as in other schools."

Melissa understood the students' long days on the bus, leaving at 7 a.m. and returning home late, because she was also a student who was away from home a great deal. However, she finally made it into the National Honor Society. She knew that obstacles were surmountable and expected the students to work when they were at school. She understood that school might be an important part of their day. Her students trusted her so much, and we could say she was so attuned to them that when I came to videotape the room, one of the students asked for a dictionary. She went up to Melissa and showed her the word *ruin*. It was not until after class that Melissa explained to me that the student was telling her that I was ruining the class by visiting and videotaping. To express that vulnerability to a teacher shows a great a deal of trust.

I asked Jennifer, "Do they need to care about art? Does it matter to you if they do well?" Even though she did not teach a core class, she responded:

> Does it matter if they care about art? It matters to me that they care about art. I take offense if they don't. I just want them to appreciate it in the sense that it has done so much for so many people. I love art. And I want everyone who comes to my class to know something about art.

## Relational Caring: Commitment

Both teachers and students showed a commitment to each other and the subject matter. Jesse, the math teacher said, "I convey commitment to them because I am always here for them." With regard to commitment to the students, Melissa commented as follows:

> Well, I think I take the initiative. I talk to students. You know, I ask them, "How was your weekend?" If I see a kid limping, I say, "Tell me what is going on." "What happened?" If someone has a broken arm, "What happened to your arm?" I ask her questions, to let her know it's okay. And also, with one student, I have actually said, "Come talk to me. I know you are quiet, and you want to talk to someone. Come talk to me."

Regarding the subject matter, she continued: "I tell them, over and over, 'This is very important. This is very important.' And they don't just need this for school; they need this for life. You need this whenever you talk to anyone in the United States."

Jennifer, the art teacher, regarded commitment as follows:

Commitment is doing what you say you are going to do . . . For example, I stayed up until 2 a.m. to finish the t-shirts for our field trip. I ironed on their names and numbers for the IC or advisory class. I asked for five bucks from each of them. It was like eight bucks per t-shirt, but I am not going to ask for, like, a five and three ones.

Denise, the science teacher, had this to say about commitment:

Yes, I do think I have a sense of commitment, but I am also practical in that I realize I can't save every single person I would like to save. I can't clothe every single student or feed every single student. I have had some heartbreaking episodes over the years. I do feel a commitment to them and tell them so, if they want to keep up a relationship with me by phone or by e-mail, or even meeting. I feel a commitment to my subject matter, but I feel like my biggest commitment is to the wellbeing of our students. And then, after that, teaching them English—and then comes my discipline.

## Relational Caring: Shrewdness/Intelligence (Intelligence Used with the Students)

Some of the comments and actions of the staff members at the Newcomer Academy showed their sensitivity to students' feelings. The staff had an awareness of how to work with students in ways that respected their dignity, but also achieved results in bringing about a behavioral change—for example, by understanding the students' weaknesses. The teaching might have also looked different. They made adjustments in language, certainly, but the math teacher also made adjustments in the way he presented the math. He looked for a way to present the equations so that the students could understand the concept visually.

Maybe they know how to work the formulas with equations, and how to solve equations because they have done it in Algebra. But they never looked for [this concept with] shapes. So I have them put it together. I let them try to put it together by themselves. But if it is something brand new that they have never seen in their lives, like congruency, then I will come in and teach them first, so they can know what it is.

The art teacher also used this technique. In addition, both the English and science teachers used visual cues and graphic organizers when presenting information to the students.

## Relational Caring: Skill/Knowledge (The Way the Material is Taught to the Students)

Again, we can see from the art teacher's description that the material was taught through the relationship, taking into account both the students' needs to be validated and their need to understand individually. Jennifer was very honest that she was not super-human. She worked better some days than others:

> I start the class together, and then I start circulating. I make it my priority to be available and not just sit by the computer. Some days I'm emotionally available, but then other days, I'm just not able. I may have a headache or cramps...

She made her room available to students who needed it as a safe space, to come during lunch or at other times during the day. When they were in class with other students, she respected that they might not be up to par. As mentioned above, some days she did not feel well. She showed that she understood with a caring gesture: "One student needed to come in during lunch, so that was cool. I patted her on the back later, when she wasn't herself."

The art teacher used the assignments to tap into the students' emotional world, accessing prior knowledge they had about themselves or the world.

> On the weekly sketch, they start getting personal and use it for emotions and stuff. I have them start out with a memory, and then we take a walk and maybe show what they see on the walk, (or write about) what they feel.

Finally, Jennifer relied on what they were doing in class in relating to the students. "I don't call the students' homes very much. Most of the phone numbers are disconnected, anyway," she said. However, once, when a student borrowed Jennifer's cell phone to call her mom, Jennifer later called the student at home and in this way, playfully connected with the student out of class. All of the teachers repeated this lighthearted way of relating to the students, and many students commented that they appreciated the good humor of their teachers: "She is always cheerful or enjoyable," said one about her teacher.

If a student resisted or didn't show an interest, Jennifer communicated with that student about attitudes.

> Some students are against the whole thing. They don't want to be here. But if they want a grade in my class, they have to buck up and do something. It is

> subjective, so I have some leeway. For those students, I try to show them that life is all about your attitude. Change your attitude a little bit, and hey, it is not hard . . . in other words, don't go around so angry.

> "One girl, Laura, was always angry, always getting into girl fights." Then she discovered that she really liked painting. "It was just like a door opening up," she told me.

Jennifer worked to keep the relationship with that student open so that she was able to find something the girl liked. The student kept coming to class and found out that not only did she like art, but that art could help her calm down a little.

She did expect the students to learn about art. That was, after all, why they were in her class, even if it wasn't a core class. "I want everyone who comes to my class to know something about art . . . Some people don't think art is a real class, so I do interdisciplinary projects with other teachers so they will know we have a place . . ." The pharaoh art project was a collaborative project between Jennifer and a history teacher, in which the students researched how the pharaohs embalmed bodies. In art class, they used colors that were indicated to be those used in the tombs. An explanation about the pharaoh encircled his head.

Melissa, the English teacher, echoed the sentiment that it was important to convey information in ways that the students would understand and that it would be a skill they would need throughout their lives.

> I tell my students sometimes to do something, such as find the main idea. They say, "Oh, we have to find the main idea?" "Yes," I say. "You have to find the main idea." This is a life skill. You know, you have to find the main idea in everything, a conversation you are having. What is the main idea? What do you need to do?

## Relational Caring: Transformational Aspect or Real Teaching

The student Raul talked about his computer teacher, who let students come in before and after school and during lunch. He helped students personally in a way that was life changing for them. The next year, without that teacher, Raul was adrift. He should have been applying for universities and scholarships, but at the time I interviewed him, no one had helped him. People may have brought it up, but not in a way that was convincing for him. I talked to many people who knew of him, but no one really knew what he had applied for, if he was a resident or not, and if he had finished his

FAFSA. There were too many other students who also needed help, and if Raul did not initiate the contact, he would get lost; and in fact, he did get lost in the shuffle.

Another student, Alicia, had talked about her dad, but the truth was that he often worked out of town and she was left in the care of her aunt, who lived next door. The aunt did not speak English or know the issues that affected Alicia as a student in an American school. In addition, she did not drive, so she could not help Alicia attend to adult issues such as taking care of absences, tickets, or other problems that arose in the teenager's life. These two students had spoken of a teacher as an adult who changed their lives, but that person, or another, needed to be there on an ongoing basis. As old issues were resolved; new ones arose.

Two years ago, I took seven students to a conference where they talked about their experience at an English language program. It was there that Olivia spoke highly of Dr. Andrade, a teacher who sat with her and helped her during her first year, when all she knew how to say were the names of colors. She was very emotional about how much he had helped her. As mentioned earlier, when I sat down with her recently, she hardly remembered him until I reminded her of his name. It's hard to say how long students hold onto experiences they have with teachers and whether these moments surface at different times in their lives, or if other people come in to take the place of formerly inspirational or transformational teachers. Olivia had spoken of talking with the principal almost every day, but perhaps the need for language support had given way to the need for emotional support and guidance about choices in the future.

An African student noted how important the Newcomer Academy teachers were in helping him adjust to the United States. The teachers related to him as friends and always asked him, "Is something wrong? Are you okay?" He later attended classes at a nearby university. What would he say if we spoke to him today? Jon, the Pakistani student, was very excited about his advisory teacher because he helped him get a scholarship, which meant a lot to him. He could see firsthand the results of the relationship he had with his teacher and the value of asking a teacher for help.

Jesse, the math teacher, believed that students feel transformative experiences when they want to share what they have learned with other students: "Real teaching is when they turn around and say, 'Isn't this like what we did the other day?' I said, 'It is just a different strategy.' They make a connection and then they, like, gasp." Jesse told me about an example of an experience when the students talked with him about a math concept they had discussed in class the previous day:

The students say, "Wait a minute. So, this number, if you put it in here, you get the same answer as if you follow this point up into the graph. These are the same representations." And they are like, "Woooo!" When that happens, they have not only learned it—they have internalized it. This kind (of experience) is what I strive for. I want them to be like, "Oh!" When they go, "Oh," I did my job. When they get the lesson that grabs them, you don't have to turn them around from their world. The lesson turns them around. The learning turns them around. "Oh, this is what he is trying to say." And they will try to get their friends to have their "Oh!" moment.

Then it makes my job easier that day because they got it, and they are excited that they got it. "This is the way it is, right, Mister? Look, look!" and then, they will go and tell someone else because they want everybody to get it the way they did. I think one reason I can help them realize it faster is that I know where they are coming from, and I know what they need to know. Like, some teachers are trying to teach equations, and they will keep them (under) a little microscope. "This is what you need to do, and this is what you need to do."

Why not show them the big picture and say, "This is what it is," and then show them piece by piece? I think that is what it is. Like, showing them, "Where are we trying to go from here?" Well, because if you get there, then this is what you need to do to get there, and this is the process to get there. If they apply what they learn from math class, it could simplify their lives. Some of them can apply the logic to their lives.

Melissa, the English teacher, told of an experience that touched her during her first year of teaching.

There is one kid who was kind of a loner. And after having talked to him a lot, I know that—I don't really know what is going on, but I know that he likes video games. He kind of acts strangely and talks about violent things sometimes. And we (teachers) have had that conversation with him, like, "Oh, you know, it's not good for you to talk about." For example, in class, the illustration of a positive thing that he did for someone was, he killed a dog. When the class watched this video about Hurricane Katrina, his response was that he was proud for all of the people who survived, but not in a way that was nice. It was an only the strong survive mentality.

And so, I guess it was about the third week, there was a student (in his class). He is very quiet, and he really needs someone to pull him up. He needed a friend. I talked to the student who was kind of antisocial. (I'll call him Pedro.) "Pedro," I said, "Can you please talk to him, Pedro?" I said, "He needs a friend." You know? And I didn't know if he would do it or not.

But then, after he finished eating, he got up, went over, and started talking to the other student. He looked at the boy's schedule, to help him go to class. I didn't know if he would do it or not, but I really wanted him to. When

I saw it, it was kind of one of those moments where I said, "Wow, I am so glad he listened to me, and even if it doesn't develop into a friendship between the two of them, at least he kind of reached out."

It would be interesting to ask that student about the incident, but usually, a teacher cannot just go and ask about such things. It might be possible with some students, but many students will just not give a direct answer to a direct question.

The art teacher had made a number of comments about how important her junior high and high school art teachers were for her. She only felt normal in their classes. In turn, Jennifer was a teacher that students mentioned when I asked them to name a favorite teacher. It takes time to develop these relationships. She says it takes time for deep moments to occur. "It takes them a full year for this to happen. I don't expect every lesson to touch them deeply. Right now we're doing perspective, and that is just a method. But then we'll switch it up with something more personal."

The following is Jennifer's comment about an experience with a student in her class: "I had a student paint her father, who had passed away...I gave her a canvas...she went to town on it...I mean, you can tell that she is going to have it forever."

Denise went through quite a bit as a student, similar to the lives of her own students, and the fact that she had siblings going through the same thing helped. In addition, her mother modeled a kind of selfless caring for others. Denise told this story:

There was horrible poverty in Mexico City. We went to church regularly and became friends with the priest. He got to know a family that lived near him, a very poor family, and they went through a horrible, tragic series of events. These eight kids were orphaned, and he worked really hard to find placements for them, but it wasn't all working out at one time. So, my mother ended up taking in these eight orphans.

Over one Christmas, we invited them to our house. And it was quite an exciting event, let me tell you. We were so annoyed with her at first. I had been away at college. I came home, and here were these eight kids, additional kids, in our house, and they had never lived in a house. I mean, they didn't know how to use the plumbing. It was really amazing. And they had never had shoes, so my mom made them clothing.

It was really an amazing thing that my mother did, because we were all—and I fully admit my part in this—we were all very negative and selfish about it, and we wanted our Christmas the way we were used to having it; you know, lots of fabulous gifts and family time. We didn't want to share any of that, but here we were forced to, with these kids that needed it so much more than we could ever have even imagined. And so it turned out to be a very enriching experience; and I have to commend my mom for going up against the whole lot of us, because we were so angry with her about it. We still keep in touch with some of these children.

The principal's father created similar teachable moments from everyday events. Every summer, the entire family went to visit relatives in a remote village in Mexico to learn about their life and to help out.

My father—and I have to go back to this, because my father took every opportunity—there was always a teachable moment. He was a very quiet man. He is a very quiet man, but he found that we had relatives in San Fernando, Mexico. And so, what he did was to pack us all up and head that way in the summer.

Well, there is no electricity, no running water—a very impoverished area. The houses are made out of mud and hay. And he would take us out there. We would go out there and live out there for a week or so, you know, every summer. And so, we had to haul water; we had to go get eggs, anything . . . harvesting the honey. We had to learn how to do all of that stuff out there; you know, herd cattle, or kill rattlesnakes. I had leeches on me from taking a bath in the river, you know, all of that when I was out there. It was all just to teach us what we had. We would get there and slaughter a pig to celebrate. That was sad for me because I loved animals. I thought, "Don't do that! I brought some hamburgers!" I even have the pictures of those experiences.

*We look through this loss,*
*For our mother's jewels.*

*Like seed pods, we*
*blow encrusted,*
*past cracked*
*dry soil.*

*Pushed by a*
*Force, to life.*

—Barbara McKinley, *Second Verse* (2006, p. 11)

# 7

# *The Practice of Care*

## *Satisfying a Longing*

*Maybe a great magnet pulls*
*All souls towards truth*
*Or maybe it is life itself*
*That feeds wisdom*
*To its youth*

*Constant craving*
*Has always been*

—Ben Mink & k. d. Lang (1991)

## What Makes a Caring Teacher?

So far the discussion has delineated different aspects of the care experience. These aspects of care have not been broken down to give a portrait of the teachers, although they do help to give us an idea about them. Rather, the attempt has been to capture the transformative experience of care. In an effort to give a fuller definition, I asked the teachers to try and describe a caring teacher. In truth, all of the examples and stories so far had that aim. We have defined care and aspects of care. Now we can try to say what those teachers look like. How would a principal, for example, know what to look for when hiring a teacher? How would a principal know that this teacher could put the students first and still maintain a stance? The balance is between giving to students while still guiding or directing them towards adulthood and a positive goal. This is a delicate balance between care and power—where both are seen as internal mechanisms as well as external, institutionalized realities.

A person is not permanently caring. A dynamic takes place between the teacher and student, and in public schools, as they are now, among the class members. The needs, interests, abilities, and inclinations of each are balanced against the other. The teacher will often put the curriculum or class's interest before the needs of an individual. The experienced teachers with whom I spoke operated their classes in such a way as to allow for contact with students as individuals, and for them to work at their individual pace and level within the guidelines that had been established by the school curriculum and expectations.

Caring is a stance or a way of relating to the students. On a good day, the teacher and students will be in synch. Some days, the teacher may be preoccupied or busy, or might have a headache; but if solid relationships have been established and the teacher is normally giving and allows a space for the student to come forward, then the students will realize the problem and be there to assist the teacher, if need be. The students will give back, or reciprocate, as long as the teacher's withdrawal is temporary. It is a natural part of the relationship, the giving and taking, one side to the other.

In a subtle way, teachers share the knowledge, expertise, and experience they have had about the subject, life, and schools; about how to maneuver within the school and within systems; and about the community around the school. In general, by helping them in their areas of interest, teachers make it clear how students can carve out a path. Within these relationships of giving and taking, the student sees how to go forward and realizes the realities that will lie ahead. This is a gift that an experienced person can give a younger one, or a student. In return, the student gives back with vitality and appreciation—in a way that motivates the teacher to continue sharing what often is kept private or in reserve, or what appears as a mystery to a student who has not yet been exposed to these experiences or worlds.

Examples are the way that Anabel described her teacher as opening a window for her: a teacher who opened the Hispanic culture to her as she talked about the Mayan culture and Isla de las Mujeras before any four-star hotels had appeared on the island. When students hear about these new worlds, they feel a sense of adventure, of something just beyond their reach; something remote yet familiar. As the student begins to step in that direction, the way seems possible. Going to college seems within reach for those who are the first in their family. Being successful seems inevitable when success has been all a student has known within the classroom.

The next steps are just those of following, when a guide or a teacher takes the lead and understands the hesitancies and issues that the students face. One teacher said: "The good students don't seem to need us as much." They don't need to be guided through the academic issues, perhaps because schools reward linear thinkers. That process may not be so automatic for those who are artists (thinking from the bottom up, as Jennifer put it), or who need to move around to learn, or who learn by any of the other modalities. Still, with help, most of these bright students will know that they can go to college and find the next steps just by looking around on their own. But will they know how to care for those who need their help? Will they naturally give to others when others show their need, or will they sit there and joke while the others are still working? And will they realize that they have things to learn from the artist, the athlete, or the politician?

Perceptive teachers understand how to help for some reason—perhaps because it was modeled, because they experienced hardships as children, or because they have been on the outside. These teachers will create a community of learners who are invested in each other, and when that heart is well opened, anything is possible. This openness is what provides the classroom environment for transformative experiences. I found that as a teacher, these experiences emerged more readily when I followed suggestions from the students or really listened to them. If I polled the students or did something they suggested, they became more motivated. When I included technology such PowerPoint presentations, video cameras, Internet research, or blogging, students also became more enthusiastic. The discipline problems often disappeared when students were motivated by the lesson or by learning. One time, the students, in groups of two, agreed on topics and were creating PowerPoint presentations. Some of the Spanish-speaking students wanted to translate a French phrase, and one of the African students had studied French at home. They were working between Spanish, French, and English. The African student, who had been somewhat isolated and desultory for a number of reasons, became an animated part of the conversation. His relationship with these new friends continued to grow, and he did not seem so moody anymore. These unpredictably beautiful experiences emerge under the care umbrella.

Each of the teachers talked about what the students could learn from their class or subject. All of the classes were not math, or art, or science, or English—but taken together, the students learned a great deal about the subject matter, about how that subject could impact their life, and consequently, about themselves.

Jesse, the math teacher, talked about why it was easy for him to be caring with his students. "I kind of have a weak spot for these kids. I don't think I would want to be anywhere else. They care about the subject because they care about the teacher. They don't want to let you down."

Jesse tied the students' learning to the relationship. They wanted to learn because they cared about him, and that was because he cared about them. Math might have been boring on some days, but the students would follow along because they knew it was for a reason, and that tomorrow it would be interesting or make sense. They could anticipate because Jesse had established the pattern in the past. They could apply the logic of math to their lives: "If I do A, B will follow." They could try to see what the consequences would be if they followed what they learned in math; if they could apply it or be shown how to apply it to their lives.

The art teacher's students learned that she would give them second chances if they needed them. From their responses to her assignments, she could decide whether the projects were worth continuing:

> I can tell by the emotions the kids have that they are not going to give me anything on that project, that I need to move on and say, "'Okay, that one was a failure. Let's throw it away and do something else that is more important." In this way, the students can learn from mistakes, if we want to call them that. They learn that just because they started something, they don't have to continue down that path. They can go back and start over. They can leave friends who are destructive, or they can walk away from something that they see is not working.

The art teacher said that she modeled the assignment and then circulated to check for understanding when she presented it to her students:

> I like to model what they are doing, their projects... (and then) I like to go out and sit with the class, you know; sit at different tables. I can't go and talk to all of them every day. But I can make my rounds for a whole week, probably, in every class."

Sometimes she would sit with them and do the same project as they were doing. "I can be at their level, and I can still model what I want from the project, so they see that, too. So they know, 'Oh, we are supposed to do this,' you know?" Because art was not a core class, Jennifer had some flexibility in how and what to teach. Even though evidence has shown that students benefit from having art and music in their lives, art is not always prescribed due to the testing environment in schools or budgetary concerns. Perhaps this oversight is a mixed blessing because then, teachers can respond to their students. "There is no curriculum. It is more, like, based on my feeling. Most people do clay at the end of the year, but I decided that I wanted to do clay now," she said.

Jennifer changed the way she gave instructions because she wanted the students to understand. She did not speak Spanish very well, so she gave her instructions in English with the assistance of visuals or body language. "I talk slower; and it's not really a language. It is more visual. I can just tell when I look across the room and they are not getting it. I can just kind of draw a picture on the board."

Melissa, the English teacher, felt that she taught her students to take responsibility for their own learning in her class. They learned how to find the main idea in reading so that they could understand what was important in a document. In this way, they were learning a life skill that would help prevent others from taking advantage of them. They were then able to talk about motives in writing and decide if that was something they wanted to believe or use in their lives.

> You have to decide whether it is something you want or not. So, to let them know, "Hey, it is not just me; it is you, too. You are the sole person responsible for your education. When it really comes down to it, you are responsible." And not in a mean way, but: "I know what it is like to be a student..."

In a general way, Denise, the science teacher, was able to articulate a definition of a caring teacher. She spoke from her many years of experience as both a teacher and a parent.

> Okay. First, it begins with mutual respect, student and teacher, and student-to-student as well. And once we have gotten those ground rules established, we pretty much go from there. We express interest in "what you did over the weekend" when you come back Monday; or "what you did for the summer." Or, if you are participating in some kind of school event, we always discuss it, or ask about it. "How is the team doing? How is the band event?" Whatever the particular activity is, ask about the event and attend as many as possible. That is kind of a good beginning for things that are outside the academic area.

And of course, my ultimate goal is to for them to learn. And they are going to want to please me a lot more when they feel that I care about them. I try to help them feel comfortable. They sit at small tables with two or three people per table, but they frequently change. I let them sit where they like at first, and then we switch every few weeks. They frequently switch groups, and they get to know everyone in the group. We learn everybody's names, and where everyone is from, at the beginning... kind of. That is good practice for English, but it is also good to get to know everybody and where they are from.

I try to think of a positive comment to give them every day. As the class gets started, we do a little warm-up activity, where I have kind of built it in such that I have to go to every student to check to see if they have done it, 10 seconds per student—and at least make one comment to each student, so at least they have had one positive interaction with me every day at the beginning of the period—at least that much. Of course, they want more than that; but that, at least. So, when you are showing me your calendar to get your stamp that you have done your work, I will say, well, you know, "How was that guitar recital yesterday? How is your sister doing? Is your mother feeling better?" Whatever, something like that.

I specifically try to focus on the family. And that is also important to our students because they are so far from their homes, their native homes. So, it is building on the family idea, really.

Denise also found out information about family or personal life that needed to be referred to a social worker or assistant principal for follow-up.

I ask questions and try to remember something about their family. "How is your Mom doing in her new job?" or, "Is your Dad better after the surgery?" Something like that. And, yes, to keep it going, to ask questions, see how things are going. Frequently, they volunteer information, too; if they have some kind of obvious injury, of course, I ask about that: "How did you scrape your arm?" or that kind of thing. And that has been a good thing for them. I have had a couple of situations where the boyfriend was beating up on the girl.

I noticed the girl had a black eye, and I wasn't going to let it go. I asked, "why, what happened?' And this just happened this past semester, actually. She just said, "Oh, I fell down." And then, her tablemates told me, "No, no, no, Miss. That is not what happened. That is not what happened. So-and-so beat her." And so, then, of course, I did not like that. And she didn't deny it. So, her friends kind of stepped in, and they felt safe enough that they could come in. It happened to be another student at our school, so it was something that we needed to deal with.

Denise also talked about how different classes would be handled differently.

> Kids that might be very energetic, they might not get to do quite as many loose activities without specific guidelines, as in some other classes. Yes, I definitely contain them in another way. I might—for example, in one class that I know—they are going to do the activities. "Okay, the materials are on the counter; here are the instructions; let's see what you can do with that." Maybe the next class that came in would be all rowdy and crazy. I would never do that because they would never get anything done. I would have to get them a little more focused. And so, yes, I do the same basic lesson but in a different manner. It is very difficult to do that because, of course, you are presenting to the group; but you have got to differentiate for the individuals, the lower achieving, and then the higher achieving students. So, that is where we—I allow them flexibility of time and change in assignments.

One way that Denise helped meet the goals of the different needs of the students was to divide students into tables of four, where they naturally worked together in groups.

> Definitely, we work in groups. And usually, if I have a brand-new student or a student that is very, very low, he is buddied up with others. Now, I don't want the buddy to do the work because I don't think that is good, either, but just someone to help them, show them what page to open the book to, or whatever, just to get them going.

Denise talked about how she encouraged students to have a sense of responsibility toward each other and establish a sense of community among each other.

> In group work, they get three grades. They get a group grade, where the whole group gets the same grade. They get an individual grade when they have fulfilled their role in the group and their assignment. Then, they get a listening grade for listening to the other groups' presentations or participating appropriately, maybe asking questions on whatever the assignment is.

In this aspect of care, of which we spoke of earlier, the teacher's practice helps the students develop a caring attitude toward each other. Here, those who understand academically assist others who may not *get it* so easily, and in so doing, they learn something in return from the students they help. They learn about their interrelatedness.

## Can Caring be Taught?

I asked teachers, school leaders, staff members, and support staff if caring could be taught. One group discussion took place among the principal, assistant principal, social worker, school registrar, and teachers. Rocio, the social worker answered the question, can caring be taught. "I think it can be modeled. Yes, I definitely believe in modeling. I think students are going to learn what we do, not always what we say; so we have to be a model for them. And it is hard sometimes."

Jesse answered this way: "Rocio said that caring could be modeled. I think caring must be felt."

Jesse often showed in his comments that he was attuned with the students. He could not only give the students' point of view but also showed the thinking that would lead a student to a new level of understanding or awareness.

### *Connecting: Satisfying the Longing*

With losses in their lives, the students have a need to connect in the classroom, as Melissa, Denise, and Jennifer's stories have shown. One day, while observing in Jesse's classroom, I started counting the number of times the students called out "Mister." In one four-minute segment, I heard "Mister" called out 22 times. It occurred many more times throughout the whole session. In the middle, some of the students would actually say his full name, as though they had remembered to say "Mr. DelaHuerta," instead of "Mister." When the lessons were hard, the students would call out for help. Jennifer said that once the students knew her as a teacher, they began to realize they did not need to call out her name. She would circulate table by table, or they could come over to her. The calmness in her room encouraged such trust.

> I've had Drawing II for a year. Most of them know my style and how I do things, so they get a lot less of "Ms. Watson." By that I mean, "Instruction, instruction," whereas the other classes need a little bit more of pushing for motivation, I guess, to get them going on stuff. The Art I classes call out to me. Drawing II knows what to do, and they are just a little bit more comfortable.

In Denise's classroom, the students heard her voice throughout the course of the day, and it soothed them. Melissa's class was smaller; students knew that she would come to them, or they could go to her.

Students want individual confirmation, over and over, day after day. Campano, in his book *Literacy and Immigrants* (2007), spoke of how loss in his class was filled with lessons that connected students to their family members, and that the connection was especially important in this vulnerable group. The immigrant population, especially, needs this attention (Bennett, 2008). When we remember the dropout rate of students and how they do not feel a connection to school, it is interesting to wonder how many students want to call out for help or attention and do not—or how many do call out but do not feel satisfied. The yearning to connect is for learning about the subject matter, but because it is so desperate in some cases, it feels that this yearning has a larger existential push behind it, and that the students want more than just the facts. The information flows through the relationship, or so Denise said; the students calling out to the teachers validates that the students want something intangible from the teacher. The teachers at this school knew the importance of answering a student's call for connection and worked to satisfy learning at this level.

## Satisfying Basic Needs in the Classroom: Pencil Policies

Students need pencils every day in school. Sometimes it seemed that a student was testing a teacher or the school in the way that took care of this basic need. At times, needing a pencil took on a more intangible aspect and seemed less a need for acquisition than a preoccupation with something indefinable, which the teachers could somehow satisfy for them. The way teachers responded to this basic daily need showed their understanding of how to work with the students in general or their perceptiveness that the request was for something besides a pencil. The way that a teacher responded could empower or disappoint, impede or enhance a student's real learning. I asked the teachers, staff, and administrators what they did when a student needed a pencil. They all understood my question because students asked every one of them for pencils on almost a daily basis.

A student in a school will usually have eight teachers each semester and interactions with other adults at the school during the day. Students will negotiate the teachers in their classrooms, and the collections of these interactions are what begin to form the culture at the school. The teachers probably never talk about something so basic as how they help students get a pencil, even though needing a pencil is often a daily occurrence. Teachers will also not realize the wide array of responses that they offer the student who must negotiate the multiple views of education on a daily basis.

Melissa, the English teacher:

> I say, "Here is a pencil." I had a box full of pencils at the beginning of the year; and now, I only have about three pencils left.

Brandy, the science teacher:

I make it a big deal if they don't have a pencil. I say, "Did you forget you were coming to school today? What else did you forget? Do you have your shoes?" They usually ask at the beginning of the school day. I tell them that I am not a store, and I'm not rich. Sometimes I tell them they need to find one. If it's somebody who usually doesn't forget one, ever, then I give that student a pencil. Sometimes I don't make a big deal out of it because there are other battles. I just want them to start working. If they don't have a pencil, then they will say, "I need a pencil," or just sit there for 30 minutes and say, "Oh, I didn't have a pencil."

Bill, the history teacher:

I thought it was kind of a headache for me at first because the kids were always asking, and I was always getting upset about it. But then, I realized how inexpensive they were, and how many we actually have in storage; there are millions of boxes. So what I did was just throw a box or two out there, and I have a space where they can grab them. And right next to it, there is a big sign that says, "Come to class prepared." And it's a non-issue. The kids know, if they need a pencil, go get it, sit down, shut up, don't make a big deal about it; just go get the pencil.

Jennifer, the art teacher:

I say, "Every day, we use a pencil in our class." That is my reaction every time. Usually, I have a box in a corner, so they know that if they need a pencil, they can go get it. But the box was stolen, so I told them I couldn't give them any pencils until the next six weeks, which is next Monday. I put out one box of pencils for the six weeks. Generally, I have two on my desk, which they can come and get. But I make a big deal of it. And I talk to them in front of the whole class: "You are drawing with a pencil. You would think you would have to bring it." I kind of joke with them, I guess.

Janice the English teacher:

I had put out about 50 pencils, similar to what you did at the beginning of the year. And within two weeks, they were all gone, so I just don't keep a lot of pencils around. Students ask me, and then I will just show them how it is. I will say, "I don't have any pencils right now." And every single time, they find a pencil somewhere. Somebody gives them a pencil, or something. Most of the time I say, "I don't have one. You've got to find one from somewhere." But I think that if I left them out every day, they would keep taking them. The same students would come in every class period without a pencil and take a new one, and I would never see that pencil again.

Abi, the English teacher:

I started making it a non-issue last year. But then, kids were running in between classes to get a pencil for the class where the teacher did make it an issue, to grab my pencils to take to the other class. I go through a lot of pencils, and then every pencil is gone. So now, I just tell them, "Hey, I am not a store. Borrow one from somebody." But it does take up time. They have got to walk around. A lot of kids will just go, "No." But then they find a person with a pencil, and then they get back to their seat. They might talk to that person when they are over there, so I am not really sure what to do at this point. I kind of like the non-issue deal, but we are going through too many of them.

Betty, the assistant principal:

Like a good parent, we are going to get on them if they forget their pencil or their homework. To me, it is a big deal. As a mom and dad, we don't want them getting lost when the kids leave us. When they leave us, and they get into these bigger schools, they get lost. Our staff is 100 percent behind them—from the support staff to the teachers—we all understand, and we all understand their needs. But when they get to the other schools, and they don't have the entire staff on board, it is difficult, and it is easy for these kids to get lost.

Celene, the science teacher:

I have a piggy bank next to a jar of pencils. Students put money in the piggy bank and take a pencil on the honor system. They come and do it on their own. It's not a big deal that way.

Rocio, the social worker:

Well, for me this is a metaphor. I remember when I first started working in schools—I was 22 years old. The pencil is an example of a resource. I could just give the student the pencil, but I don't believe in this. I said, "No, don't just 'give them something' because then, they will be back tomorrow for the same thing."

Anabel, the principal:

I want to use this story as an example. I went to Mexico once, and the kids stood on the side of the road and put out their hands. And you felt with your heart, "Oh, my gosh. I have $100, and this student has nothing. Let me give him a dollar." And the tour guide said, "Don't you dare do that to my people." I didn't understand what he meant. He explained, "You are ruining an entire culture of people by handing out something for nothing." So, I haven't believed in something for nothing after that day. I believe that if you want a pencil, you have to put something up here while I lend you my pencil. If you don't have one or can't afford one, then I will sure buy one for you. But after that, I have bought you a pencil, and you had better *have* that pencil—something for something. What is it that you are going to give me while you borrow my pencil? Because I expect my pencil to come right back here. You know why? Because tomorrow, you won't have one, and you will have to go through that same routine. So, if we are into a routine—and I don't want gold rings or necklaces, or anything; I just want something—put your backpack up here while I lend you my pencil. Some students like that routine, just for attention.

Jesse, the math teacher:

At the very beginning, I would be handing them out and telling them that I need them to—if they need another one, if theirs is real small, then I will give them another one. There is no problem. But if they keep losing it, or if they are the type of student that it keeps happening over and over and over and over, then I start charging them $1.00 per pencil. And if they forget to give me my pencil back, then I forget to give them their dollar back.

Roy, the coach:

I think it goes along with what everybody is saying. I think Jesse is saying that different types of students are treated differently. I would do this if a student were chronic and habitual: "Hey, I forgot my pencil. I am not going to do my work." By golly, then I say, "I've got a pencil here for you to do your work." A lot of times, I think they come in and say, "I need a pencil" to get out of doing work. Well, you know what? I am going to do the opposite: "Here is a pencil. You know what? Keep this pencil."

It is interesting that every teacher had a policy or had created a way of working with this daily need in the classroom. Jesse was articulate and showed a progression in the process or implementation of his policy. Jesse modified his policy a little each time he retold it to me. When I observed his classroom, and a student asked him for a pencil as he walked by, Jesse answered, "Use a pen" as he continued to walk to the student who needed help with a math problem. What we say we do and what we actually do among the fast-paced demands of the classroom may vary. The request for a pencil was triaged against the need of a student asking for help with a math problem. As Jesse walked by and answered, his tone of voice conveyed, "Why bother with that? Don't you know what to do in that situation? I'm going to help someone who came prepared to learn."

Often, multiple demands are placed on a teacher at the same time, and the teacher has to make split-second decisions that might not satisfy everyone.

Students respond to the way that we approach them, and they respond, in turn, to others in the way that they are treated. In this example with pencils, there are almost as many ways to handle a daily issue in a classroom as there are teachers. From the way we act, students come to know us. Our actions show if we care or not, and students react to these action.

*Of the Land*

*His message flows through my body,*
*my bones, my heart, my fingers,*
*my pen even, moving*
*to realize unfinished dreams—*
*flowing through my veins*
*like the liquid fuel found*
*underground after his passing;*
*heard in the air*
*as the sound of a pumping derrick,*
*the heartbeat of the land,*
*thrown out as*
*a whispering desire,*
*pulsing through*
*my veins and pen,*
*flowing like the Ganges*
*towards a place of peace.*

—Barbara McKinley, *Second Verse* (2006, p. 27)

8

# The Practice of Personal Advocacy

## Meeting Social, Emotional, and Personal Needs of Students

*I was wondering where the ducks went when the lagoon got all icy and frozen over.*
—J. D. Salinger (1991, p. 13)

## What is Advocacy?

Typically, we think of advocacy in a school as the role of the social worker or school psychologist. We know from sociologists such as Stanton-Salazar (1997) and Valenzuela (1999) that with marginalized populations such as adolescent immigrants, more individuals in the school need look out for the students' needs if their needs are to be met. Just as everyone needs to become a language or reading teacher in a high school with large populations of language learners, so, too, every teacher needs to be an advocate (Bennett & Jaradat, 2011).

*Care & Advocacy: Narratives from a School for Immigrant Youth,* pages 93–107
Copyright © 2012 by Information Age Publishing

With schools that use advisories, one teacher at every school can be the caretaker of about 24 students (Cushman, 2005). The argument is that if one person cares about and believes in the students, it will be enough to help them complete their high school studies. So many pulls and outside forces can work against the students' finishing that more than one adult may be needed, especially if the students must take care of their families' financial, medical, or familial responsibilities. It takes many adults to understand these tensions in a student's life. These adults need a system to be put in place for them to communicate their concerns about the students, and then that system must become adaptable to those needs. It is not enough to say that a student must adapt to the system. Sometimes the system needs to bend and accommodate as well, especially if many students show the need for it to be bent.[1]

---

## Personal, Emotional, and Social Aspects of Immigrant Adolescents[2]

Adolescent students have emotional, social, and academic needs. New immigrant adolescents, in addition to ordinary adolescent angst and related issues, face academic challenges as they learn a new language and make cultural adjustments in a new country that may not be ready to embrace them. In order to help stabilize the emotional life of the adolescents, successful teachers generally recognize human nature, understand youthful attitudes, and are in tune with the playfulness of youth. When these personal, social, and emotional aspects of the students are met, the adolescents are much better able to meet the academic challenges of the classroom. Compounding the academic and emotional realities of adolescence, immigrant students have experienced the loss of country and family members upon their arrival in the United States, especially the loss of their grandparents or extended families. Teachers, or even the students themselves, do not always completely understand the dimensions added to an adolescent immigrant's life. All of these elements can become barriers in the educational setting if their importance is not understood, or if these needs are not addressed. Conversely, if teachers understand their importance, these barriers can become opportunities for *caring* relationships to develop and for learning to take place. In addition, students may have requirements that are basic human needs, personal or familial needs (economic, medical, or some other issue), or intercultural social dynamics that teachers should take into account. At the Newcomer Academy, the teachers empathized with students by drawing from the experiences of their own adolescence.

## Students' Loss of Family, Grandparents, or Country

Many of the students had lived with their grandparents because their parents either worked or had already come to the United States. Alicia wrote about how important a relationship could be to a teen, and what it was like to meet her father for the first time in her life when she was 15 years old.

> Someone who has made a big impact on my life is my dad. He got me out of a way of living that was killing me. He changed my life completely in a positive way. After I was born, my grandma took care of me. All of my aunts, uncles, and cousins were jealous of me because my grandma stopped paying attention to them. She dedicated her care to me, so they didn't like me.

Students also spoke of the importance of their grandparents and often mentioned them without being asked. Many of the students had been raised by a grandmother or grandfather when their parents came to the United States to make money, or even while they worked in their own country. When the students came to the United States, they left these caregivers to join other family members. Alicia describes her experience:

> Next year, I think I am going back to Mexico. I don't want to, but I have to. My grandma raised me, and now she is very sick. There are two things I'm thinking about. If I stay here, I can have a better future; but if she dies, I'm going to feel guilty. I don't know if I can help her, but I still want to be with her.

Other students spoke fondly of their grandparents. Jon, a student from Pakistan, said, "I remember about my grandfather. He died in 1997. He used to farm. In the whole family, I was the closest one to him."

As Raul, a student from Mexico, wrote, "I would ride my bicycle to my grandmother and grandfather's farm every weekend. I'd ride along the road and go there alone."

Anna, a very strong and intelligent student from Cuba, also remembered and missed her grandparents: "I think about my grandparents all the time. I talk to them. I think about them because I used to live with them before I came here. My mom and dad lived across the street. I lived with my grandparents because my mom and dad worked."

Martine, a student from Honduras, spoke wistfully of the times he spent with his grandmother:

> When I think about my childhood, I think about my grandma because I didn't grow up with my mom. I grew up with my grandmother. She was the

only one that was supporting us at that time because my mom came to the United States when I was four years old... My grandmother passed away last May... I think about her a lot. She was one of the influences in my life.

The extended family, the importance of family elders, and the wisdom that they carried were important parts of childhood memories for these students. Grandparents have an understanding of children from having seen their own children grow. They seem to do better with this second chance at relating to children because they might understand what is important and know how to make children feel special. Grandparents know about loss, as they have seen friends, neighbors, and even children pass on. The way they relate to others has been refined, perhaps because their love is not so judgmental. Whatever the reason, these students talked about their grandparents a great deal. This special bond might be why abuelos, or grandparents, held a special place in the school culture and experience. Grandparents and their grandchildren are naturally playful in their relationship.

The staff members at the Newcomer Academy instinctively knew how to come forward and fill that role in the lives of the students. Ms. Terry talked about her maternal role with students:

Oh, they are like my kids. They call me "Grandma." And they come to me for everything. I tell them, "You have to go to this person. You have to go to this other one," but they are away from home and they miss that maternal touch. Some of them have been raised by their grandmas in Mexico. So, when they see me, they relate to me as a mother figure, grandma figure. And they go, "Grandma"—they call me Grandma. Abuela, Abuela! Abuelita! And they are close to me. But I have to be firm with them, too because, you know, sometimes they want to take advantage with their grandmas.

Ms. Terry showed her sense of humor and playfulness in the way she related to the students. She was available, attuned to the students, and commanded respect from them as she filled a loss they felt in their lives.

The science teacher, Denise, spoke about her transnational experiences as a child. She had a strong family, and because all of her siblings were going through the same experience, that made it easier. Being the oldest may have caused her to brush away some of her experiences because she had to help siblings deal with their transitions. Despite the movement between different school systems, she always had a stable financial base with her family, which helped to reduce some of the anxiety of the moves her family made. In addition to her childhood experiences, when her daughter had medical problems and almost died later on, Denise reached a turning point in her life. She no longer wanted to be with students who displayed privilege and nonchalance towards or unawareness of the suffering in the world.

> I was at Sam Houston High School, I want to say, eight years. My daughter became ill, so I left. And then I worked at the university for a while, part-time, supervising student teachers during that time. When my daughter was better, and I could come back to work, I didn't feel the same about Sam Houston anymore. It was completely different. It was the strangest thing. I'd been through a life-and-death situation with my daughter—she had leukemia—and so she had almost died many times. I went through so many intense things; and when I came back to the privileged, rich kids, I just couldn't take it. The same things that I had embraced before suddenly irritated the heck out of me, and I just couldn't take it. I decided that it wasn't a fit for me. I wanted to relate to students on a deeper level. It was my exact same classroom, the exact same situation, and everything that they had had before that didn't work.

## Personal Needs[3]

At the Newcomer Academy, the teachers, staff, and administration understood the personal needs of the students. The social worker was involved in many conversations and meetings with the teachers. Hearing her voice calling for students over the loud speaker was a common part of the school day. At another school, these announcements may have seemed like an interruption, but this school regarded taking care of the personal needs of students as vital.

Rocio, the social worker talked about the personal needs of students:

> As a social worker, yes, relationships are very important with students. I think the better the relationships that we build with students—the more personal we can make learning—the more productive students will be...The more open they'll be to learning, the more comfortable they're going to be with their teachers, the more comfortable they're going to be about asking questions, and the better they're going to participate.

> For me, I have different kinds of relationships since this is such a small school. Sometimes I'm the hall monitor, so the relationship can be administrative. And then at other times, I am sitting with them one-on-one, and they are telling me their deepest, darkest secrets. So, the relationships definitely vary. I think it is important for me, especially at the beginning, to know everybody's names and call them by name. At the very minimum, I want to have that kind of social relationship and then build from that.

Anabel, the principal, clarified how important she felt it was for teachers and staff to take responsibility for multiple roles with the students:

> The first year, I asked that all support personnel do hall duty and work in the cafeteria during lunch. One person was hesitant. She said, "I am supposed to be a nurturing person, not a disciplinarian, so I can't go out there and do that." But in my mind, a healthier relationship with a student is one where you can do both. To say to a student, "I am sorry, but you can't do that," and also, "I love you, and yes, I will keep your secrets." It takes that well-rounded relationship for a person to respect you. And so I insisted that this person come out and do these things because that is a much healthier relationship than just being a yes-person.

Jesse, the math teacher, gave his opinion:

> I think that relationships are really important—that is, speaking of positive relationships—of trying to get students to participate or be engaged in the classroom, whether it is a boring class or an exciting class. If you build a relationship with students, where they respect you and respect what you are going to say, then at any given point, you could point out to them that they are being rude, and they will sit back and say, "You know what? I'm sorry. I'm sorry I did that. I didn't mean it." And feel bad about it. Having that relationship and that feedback makes them feel accountable for their actions, and pay attention to what I am saying—and for them to be able *to* pay attention.

Denise, the science teacher:

> Adding to what Jesse has said, I think that this is part of our job as teachers: to teach them. Not only do we teach them our content areas, but we also teach them or try to model good relationships. And if they are doing something rude, then I feel it is our responsibility to point that out and tell them how they could do it better. So I think—back to the responsibility aspect—I think that the relationship is even more important than the content because the content follows the relationship.

When asked if teaching students to be caring or understanding of others is a part of being a teacher—an important part of education—Denise said, "Yes, it's essential."

## Familial Needs (Economic, Medical, or Other Issues)

With this population of students, who come from cultures where the immediate and extended family and its needs are seen as primary, taking care of those personal needs is of vital importance. Anabel, the principal comments:

> I've noticed something, using the skill of observation that I have picked up. I've noticed that adults are also guilty of not being able to find the strengths in others. Sometimes it's hard to find the good in another adult; and when we work in such a small school, it's very easy to see the faults of other people. It's hard to look for the positive and overlook the negative. We tend to be quick to put it out there, and then the adults start having problems. And so what I most like about this school, most of the time, is that we have grown accustomed to providing constructive criticism for each other; and one way or another, it's going to come out. It will have to come out sooner or later because we are such a small school. And I am not going to let it go on and on, even if it means we are going to have to come together and see it for what it is, head-on. And this is not always comfortable for people.

Betty, the assistant principal:

> With adults, whether we see it or not, our behavior directly affects the relationships and the type of work we are doing with our students. It's difficult because the students see everything; they feel everything. We think that we are hiding it, but we aren't hiding it. And the tensions build, and it trickles down in our work.

Roy, the coach:

> Well, I can tell you, just on my part, that last year, I didn't belong to a team since I'm a coach. So I was out of the loop, so to speak. And this year, I know what's going on with the school and can actually go to another facility and talk about our school—and feel comfortable with what I say and how I say it. I can feel that I know what I am talking about—only because I am more informed this year than I was in the past.

Ana, the school registrar:

> Even though as the school registrar I'm not on any particular team with the faculty, a lot of teachers do include me in what is going on with a particular student. Or, we include each other because we have conversations with our co-workers. If one faculty or staff member is having an issue with a student, chances are that we would involve somebody else.

Anabel, the principal:

I need to point out something. With regard to the matter of confidentiality, it is different here than it is at other places. Rocio tries her very best, but I don't believe in that confidentiality when it comes to the nurturing of a student. Once we establish an environment that cares for students, then it's important for each of the adults, responsible adults, to know what's going on with that student because it totally impacts how that student behaves in class. And if a teacher doesn't know the background about what's happening, we'll be working in the dark. We are just stabbing in the dark. For example, if a student is having a crisis with a pregnancy, she's not thinking about math. She's thinking, "Oh, my gosh! I am underage. I don't want this baby. The father of my child has left me, and here I am in an adult situation with no way out. I don't have any money, but I'm Catholic, so I can't give this baby up. What is he talking about denominators up there?"

Jesse, the math teacher:

I had another instance when there was one student in the morning that would stand by the stairs. One morning, I just got mad at him because I always saw him there, and I tried to send him to the cafeteria with all of the other students. I said, "Why are you here?" Later in the team meeting, I told everybody, "This student just doesn't want to go to the cafeteria when he is supposed to go. He stays in the hall all the time." They told me he had a problem walking; he had a walking problem. Now I know why he stands where he stands.

Rocio, the social worker:

I think one of the situations that we have here is very unique, and it's something that I've not seen in other settings. We are very much like a family. We get on each other's nerves. Sometimes we hurt each other's feelings. But we genuinely care about each other, and we back each other up. When it comes down to it, we are going to take care of each other, and we're going to back each other up. And so, yes, occasionally—especially in the stressful environment, we are dealing with students, with deadlines, with limited resources—and we get frustrated, and it's real easy to take it out on each other. I tell my students, "It is like that saying, 'We hurt the ones we love.'" It's a lot easier to take out our anger or frustration on somebody that is still going to be there and care about us afterwards than it would be on a complete stranger.

I want to say, as a parent and as a social worker in a school. I think we have to show students that we are not perfect. We have to show them that yes, we make mistakes. And, you know, it does happen. I think by showing them that we can own up to when we make a mistake, that we do take responsibility for the choices we may have made that weren't the best choices. So we teach the students by modeling for them how to deal with similar situations.

## Jesse, the math teacher:

When I came here, I thought some of the things that people from here did were stupid. When I was driving, I would think, "This guy just let me in into the front of the line when I am on the expressway. Why did he do that? Back where I'm from, we would fight to get in front, and nobody would let anybody in. But then I noticed that when people would let me in, and they were kind enough to do that, then when I was not in a hurry and someone was trying to get in, I would move back and let somebody get in front of me. And that wasn't because some driver modeled it; it was because I had felt it.

For students, it's the same thing. You show them kindness or give them a break, and they think you are being dumb for giving them high points, or giving them that one point so that they could get the 70 on their test and pass. And I'll talk with them about it. But then, the next time around, I might say to a student, "You know what? I did this for you, and you let me down. You just turned around and walked away." The student is like, "Oh, wow! I can't believe I did that." They feel it. Once they feel it, then they know what you were trying to model to them.

## Ana, the school registrar:

Respect needs to be earned, not demanded. And going back to how to even develop relationships, a lot of times we can start by just telling them, "Good morning," by validating their existence that day.

## Anabel, the principal:

I have to deal with these things every day. Last week, we had three boys who were tardy, and I was very upset with them. The teacher had asked them to wait outside the room, but one just got up and left. I started talking with him, and he kept on snickering. So I thought, "You know, this student is in trouble!"

"You call your mother right now, and tell her to get up here right now. Do you care about this?" And he goes, "Whatever."

"Well, if you don't," it was quick for me to say, "do you know that I can throw you out?" . . . and I went on and on. I left it at that, not thinking it would even affect him because with other students, you can say that and they will say, like, "Yeah, right, whatever." This student listened to every single word I said and went home and cried and cried and cried. He didn't eat for two days. His mother came in, and she cried, and we all cried.

I wasn't really going to throw him out, but he was listening. He thought, "Tomorrow, I am going to be out in the street, and my whole life is going down the drain."

I had to apologize. I told him, "I don't apologize to you for being upset with you. I apologize because I used the wrong words." You know, "You are not going to be out in the street tomorrow." But he is still going to do what he wants to do because his mind is set to do this. I'm not sure my apology is going to change his behavior. In fact, it may even make him think I am a little bit weak. But it was necessary for me because I made such a big thing of it.

Denise, the science teacher:

I want to make a comment on what Anabel just said. This is a perfect example of a caring environment—that the principal is willing to go out and say, "I am sorry for the words that I chose, or whatever it is."

Anabel:

I went to his house . . . on Halloween night . . .

Denise:

It was quite humorous. She was dressed as Pocahontas. It was the topic of many conversations among the teachers, and we know that it really did affect her. We respected that; as a faculty, we respected that.

Anabel:

Well, you know, I called that family that night. And then, the next day I pulled the student out of class. He still wasn't willing to listen to me. Although he looked at me and heard the words I was saying, my words really didn't mean anything to him. He did not feel that. He did not care. But it was said, and that is what mattered. It was like when you dye clothes and they turn that color, there was no way back. Now, the only way back with that student is that I had the opportunity a few days later. He came in on a different referral, so I got to talk to him and understand why he was acting the way he was.

Then, I found out that his dad had died, and a lot of other details from his family life. When I had said, "I'm going to throw you out in the street," he thought, "Go right ahead, because the rest of the world has, too." At that point, nothing mattered, no matter what. So, I don't know that I've totally resolved the issues with this student, but I think he is thinking about what happened; and that, really, truly, he believes that I wish it would have been a different situation.

## Displaying Human Nature

It is hoped that all teachers will be student centered, but even when they have the intention, it may not always be possible. This hold true especially if teachers do not have the skills or experience to adapt materials for language learners, are not confident in dealing with a student's anger or cannot pinpoint the source of it, or do not have insights into a student's discomfort. After all, teachers are human. As Jennifer, the art teacher, said, "I may have a headache that day, or my child has been sick, and I can't focus as I usually can."

At times, teachers do not understand that they have blind spots or parts of themselves that keep them from seeing, or that they themselves are a part of the problem. Teachers and students alike all want to be accepted for their strengths and honored for what they do right. Teachers want students to understand that they are trying and that they care, even if they do not always know how to communicate it. Students also want to be accepted for their intentions and not severely punished for youthful inattentions. We are all human, and we are all a part of the problem—or solution.

The factors that enhance caring relationships are often related to the factors that impede the development of care in schools. In assessing the issues around a barrier, teachers and students are then able to change that barrier into an access or bridge through open and *caring* relationships. The problem and solution are enmeshed and intertwined and are therefore dealt with together. Some aspects of human nature that might interfere with developing caring relationships might include teachers having a bad day, misunderstanding students' love of play, or being unaware of youth consciousness.

## Playful Nature of Being Young

When students talked about their childhood in their home country, they spoke of being outdoors, running, and playing. Their memories of childhood were crowded with images of people. Raul, a Mexican student, said:

> Back in Mexico, I used to have fun every single day. I used to walk out of my house and see kids having fun, and that is something I just don't see here at all. I used to play soccer with my school buddies every day; we used to search for rivals so we could play and have fun beating that other team. It was just great.

Anna, a Cuban student, said, "I used to play baseball with the boys . . . with my cousin. Everyone played. Our neighbors were much closer together there."

Eduardo, another Cuban student, commented that he and his friends did things in groups: "Every day, we went swimming at a river by my house. Since I was four, I was in the water . . . I was never in my house. I just went there to sleep. We played, and as a group, we did things together."

The teacher, Jesse, remembered his own childhood and spoke of the importance of outdoor play in his own life:

> We have a lot of memories from our childhood. We grew up in a neighborhood where all the kids growing up were the same ages. So all the kids would get together, and in the seasons, we'd play baseball; we'd play football; we'd play war with little contraptions that we'd make with slingshots.

Overwhelmingly, the boys spoke of play more often than the girls. However, one of the girls said that she always played with the boys, "In Cuba, I was a boy." It may be that the boys were more likely to play outside.

Other students commented about how they were often together with others in social settings when at home. Martha, an Ethiopian student, recalled her times with their friends and family members with fondness, "I remember spending my time with everybody else. Mostly, we spent our time with our friends. It was a social life. It was our culture. Mostly, we spent time together. The family spent time together, too."

The importance of play and socializing with friends was apparent with many of the students. The Euro-American values of individualism, competitiveness, isolation, and self-determination were not seen in the values of these students, whose lives had been filled with family and friends. These social contacts were important factors for their well being. The playfulness of these students in the halls and classrooms can be viewed as an extension of this social contact. At the Newcomer Academy, student work that hung on the walls appeared in science projects that described the cell in terms of a 15-year-old party cell, or the Mexican cell.

When the students entered the halls, their faces matched the poignancy of their student work. This school had a feeling of life in the hallways, where students walked in twos and threes with arms intertwined and that glow in their faces of which Noddings (2003) spoke. They moved down the halls in clumps and clusters, laughing as they stopped to talk with friends.

Teachers who are overly strict in the classroom might try to stifle the students' playfulness. I saw many of the teachers take advantage of the students' inclination towards socializing and group activity to enhance the learning environment. In Jesse's case, he used this playfulness to maintain order. For example, when one of the boys wore his sunglasses, Jesse said nothing but motioned for him to put the glasses on his head as he walked by. He just motioned for the glasses to go from the face to on top of the head. The student said something about the sun being so bright, and Jesse motioned again. All of this exchange, meanwhile, occurred in passing. The boy moved the sunglasses up and then off, putting them on his desk. Jesse did not punish the boy; he only had to make it clear in a playful way that he needed to take off the sunglasses.

Another example of how a teacher used the group consciousness to create a learning environment was in the science teacher's class, where all of the tables had groupings of three to five students together. The girls worked quietly while they talked with one another; the act of learning was tied in with this socializing. Five boys sat at a table together and entertained each other with little jabs or pokes as they went through the lesson. One of the boys came over to clarify the assignment with Margaret, and others moved to different tables to check answers or talk with other students. The students liked working together, and Margaret understood their need to talk and work in groups.

Yet another class involved the students' socializing as they learned. In the English class, the students were in rows when Melissa explained the lesson, but they moved their desks together in random ways as they began to write. One group was in a cluster of four students; the others were in pairs or worked alone. The students liked to joke with Melissa as she explained the lesson. Students were to go to the blackboard and draw an illustration to show that they understood the concept she was explaining: "Draw an eye; draw a dialogue bubble; draw your feet." The students drew these images on the board and had fun illustrating the ideas. In general, the students and teachers went about their work in a lighthearted way.

The teachers took advantage of the students' mirth and let it set the tone for the classroom and the working groups.

## Teachers' Empathy From Their Own Backgrounds

The teachers showed that they understood youth and their issues from their own backgrounds. Teachers achieved success by tuning in to the contemporary youth consciousness; they also adapted lessons by remembering their own experiences as students. Jesse, the math teacher, recommended an important quality for a new teacher: "With this population, I would, first of all, get a person that is not easily intimidated. Once these kids see intimidation, then they run all over you. Pretty much any kids, with this group especially, have to be street-smart."

Jennifer, the art teacher, said she skipped as much school as possible. Knowing how easy it is for students to feel shut out, she wanted her class to be inviting: "At school, I didn't go to many classes, but I did go to my art classes. I was the kid they found in corners. 'Oh! Oh, yes, I am supposed to be in class?' I was never good in school. That's why I kind of laugh daily that I am a teacher now."

Early in Denise's career, she taught at Robert E. Lee High School. Her brother, who had just moved back from Mexico with her family, was also there as a student. Denise showed that she understood the circumstances in which a student might not like attending school. She and her brother would empathize with each other when they met in the middle of the day:

> My family had just come back from Mexico—and my brother entered (school) as an 11th grader. He was bused to Lee. He came from this private school in Mexico City, very elite, where 100 percent of the kids went to college. We would meet in the hallway, because I was a traveling teacher. I hated not having a classroom. Both of us hated it so much, we would go into a room and say, "What can we do?" and cry to each other.

Melissa, the English teacher, experienced firsthand what it felt like to be judged by teachers because of appearance. She was a smart student who liked to be *cool* and moved between different groups of students. Teachers tried to peg her as a certain kind of student because of the way she dressed.

> I hit puberty when I was 14. I was very much a late bloomer. This was when grunge was in style. Some kids wore all black: the black T-shirts; the big, black, baggy jeans. The *Second Coming of Goth*. And so, that is what I wore. It was to hide the fact that I didn't have breasts yet.

Anabel, the principal, talked about being excited about school in Comal, her hometown. She worked with the newspaper and was very active in school. She attended a university in Samuelson on a communications scholarship. Before long, she dropped out because she did not feel a connection with the school.

> I hated everyone and everything that had to do with journalism at the university. It was impersonal. They were rude. And everyone was, you know, dog-eat-dog. The teachers were insensitive. The school was very competitive. I hated it. I had straight A's the year before I went to college. But I failed when I went to college.

The principal set the tone for the school. Anabel, in understanding that competitiveness and an impersonal environment could be detrimental, knew how they could affect a student, especially one from a warm culture that likes to do things together. She hired people, either deliberately or instinctively, who showed that they understood adolescents and their need to connect. She supported her teachers in the same way.

> *O body swayed to music, O brightening glance,*
> *How can we know the dancer from the dance?*
> —Yeats, *Among School Children* (1970, p. 111)

# 9

# The Practice of Advocacy

## Working as Academic Advocates for Students

*Some people think that they are helping kids*
*when they feel sorry for them.*
*I don't feel sorry for them.*
*I've got to push them.*

—Anabel Garza, Principal, Newcomer Academy

## Academic Advocacy

Academic advocacy is what we normally think of as a teacher's role. Nonetheless, teachers may want their students to succeed without always considering that their success may look different than the expectations of the school system. For instance, many of the adolescent immigrants needed to work outside of their home, so why couldn't the school strike up a partnership with a community college to create a five-year program? If the students could graduate with a certificate for semi-skilled work, then they might be more motivated or able to complete their high school coursework.

*Care & Advocacy: Narratives from a School for Immigrant Youth,* pages 109–118
Copyright © 2012 by Information Age Publishing
All rights of reproduction in any form reserved.

The teachers at the Newcomer Academy wanted to develop relationships to teach character education; they expected their students to know the subject matter, communicate effectively, understand or learn about language learning needs, and appreciate cultural differences.

## Understanding the Teacher's Perspective: Being an Academic Advocate

One of the first rules of academic learning is to develop relationships with the students. According to the principal, although learning was very important, learning character development was one of the first academic lessons:

> I had an experience at a science academy with students who were top notch, and what I found a lot of times was that it's all about me. Although they were very intelligent students, very intelligent students—there's no doubt that they are going to be successful in academics—but I have seen what happens to them as they come out into the world as adults. Some of those people aren't able to function in their own jobs because they are so self-centered and so insensitive to others. I compare it to having a lot of money. I can have a lot of money and do whatever it is that I want, but if I don't have good friends to do it with me, then what is the joy of being able to achieve some of those things? And so for us, establishing these relationships with students is essential. It's a respectful relationship, but at the same time, it's tested. Sometimes we have to teach them things.

> This very morning, I had a situation with a young lady who thought she was right, and the teacher was wrong. From her world—she was not willing to go out of her box, even to consider whether the teacher was right or wrong. *She* was right. And it was my job to help her see that "You are 50 percent of the problem because this teacher also has a side—you know, this is her side, and that is your side." So, my job wasn't a very nice job this morning because I also had to tell the parent, "You are doing her a disservice by coming to her defense in a situation that you don't understand yet." So, it doesn't always look nice. We aren't always smiling; we aren't always happy. It's also teaching very serious skills that last a lifetime.

When asked if her work is about moral or ethical development, she says, "Character building." Asked about the need to keep class going while also attending to the students' needs, Anabel said:

> I go through this every single day. And one of the ways I manage is to set up the classroom in such a way that the students know where to find out what they are supposed to do. So, if I am tied up working with one student over here, who is perhaps a problem child, but another student is ready to move

on—then that student knows where to go to figure out what it is she is supposed to be doing; it's written on the board, or some such thing.

## High Expectations

Felicia, a student from Mexico, talked about the things she likes in a classroom and the importance of teachers expecting the students to work to their full capacity. The students do not respect teachers who ask too little of the students:

> He is very interactive; he would explain things so that the students can understand in his class. I mean, he had a lot of activities with his students. Mr. Castillo teaches geometry and algebra very well. I mean, he teaches you exactly how to solve all the steps of an equation. And he expects you to learn them. He would ask you if you understood or not. But if we didn't understand, he told us that we could go and ask him about our problem. Sometimes we did, and sometimes we didn't; but generally, I think I did my best. I think that teachers need to push the students a little bit more—and be a little bit stricter with them. Because they think that teachers are stupid. If you are nice, they think that you are stupid.

> I have a lot of teachers that are strict, but they can also be good friends with the students in the class . . . Like, Mr. Walker. He is very strict, but we can be his friend. I was paranoid the first time I went and asked him. But he is very funny; he is very nice. Yes, if a teacher is strict, that doesn't have to be, "Ah, he is a bad person." No, it is just like he wants the best for us; he wants for us to give more than we expect we can.

This particular student was not a strong student but continued in school and graduated that year, even though school in the United States was hard and her command of English needed to improve. She expressed the need for teachers to be friendly but strict. Jesse mentioned the same thing, "Teachers need to be strict but not mean."

Anna, a student from Cuba, and Olivia, a student from El Salvador, explained that school was different for them at Lee High School in the United States, as opposed to school in their home country. Both of these girls graduated and went to a nearby university:

> There are so many things that are not explained. We have to do everything in order to understand. We did everything together in our country, but here, school is boring. In each class, we have different people. In El Salvador or Cuba, we had the same students in all of our classes. The students moved to the different classes together.

Here, we don't know the teachers, either. We don't know our neighbors. It's a little sad. I like my math teacher . . . because she always worries about us. If you don't understand what she is talking about, she spends more time with you. She explains things to you. Most teachers don't care. They just give you the work and don't care if you don't get it. They sit at the computer. That's what they always do. Some walk around. Not all of them. They don't motivate us; they really don't.

We want them to explain, to take time to help us learn. There are some teachers that help us. That's what they're supposed to do. At the Newcomer Academy, they all explained. They all cared very much. If you didn't pass a test, then you could go to their class and make up the work. It's good when they push us hard.

Eduardo, a student from Cuba, also expressed the need for teachers to care. "Yes," he said, "it is important to think that a teacher cares about me because then, I don't want to miss that class. Because you know he will show you something you need to know. I'm not crazy about school . . . but it's a better option than others."

As seen from these passages, the students know if they feel cared for. This is the challenge of teaching. Different students respond in so many different ways. Having extra adults, such as *los abuelos* or teachers' aides, helped. From having a variety of adults with whom they interacted, the students could get the feedback they were used to receiving.

Raul, a student from Mexico, expressed his feeling that a teacher should show an interest in the students' learning:

This teacher would teach you as much as he knew. He would make an entire class just for one student to learn, if this student really wanted to. He would even learn new stuff to teach us. He helped a lot of the students get into college. He would help any student that needed and wanted his help. He was about learning, fun—and he was interesting.

One day as I was observing a social studies class at Lee High School, some Newcomer students appeared in the class. They were more advanced and ready to take one or two academic courses. Because the Newcomer Academy was housed in the same building, Lee High School accommodated the students by allowing them to transition into some of their classes including this pre-AP world history class. It was hard merely to observe the students when they asked me for help. The Lee High School students talked and went through their worksheets easily. They seemed to have learned how to skim for the information and fill in the blanks on the sheet that they turned in at the end of class. This sheet was recorded in the teacher's grade book for the daily grade, and the worksheet was what the students needed to study in order to pass the tests.

The Newcomer students who transferred could not skim so easily through the dense text. They did not know to look for the titles, pictures, and other clues in the text that could give them answers without reading every word. They thought they were supposed to read and understand every word. Skimming itself was hard if the vocabulary was not comprehensible. Instead of observing the class, I began to sit with them and tried to help them glide through the worksheets by looking for answers. At first, they had a hard time accepting that this was learning. They wanted to learn the material or understand, and not just fill in the sheet. When I worked with them, the teacher became a little nervous. She began to spend more time with the newcomers. They were clustered together at the back of the room, where it was hard to hear. I suggested that they be dispersed with the other students in the class and sit towards the front of the classroom.

Barriers are opportunities if viewed through the lens of a caring teacher or the ethic of care. The teachers' availability to their students' needs, their attunement to the issues, and their openness to act and be responsive are all behaviors that result from their caring attitude and attention. When teachers can communicate their concerns and are authorized to work with others to resolve issues that are often common to other situations, then a positive process begins. This process translates into an encouraging school culture and educational setting that is conducive to learning, which creates positive memories for all involved.

## Knowing the Subject Matter

Students need teachers who are available and attuned to them. They also need teachers who can teach them effectively as a result of their subject matter competence. All of the teachers showed this understanding and knowledge of skills in their interviews and the way they taught their classes. They had a passion for their subject matter and a love of learning. Jennifer, the art teacher became a student with her students, drawing with them:

> I like to go out and sit with the class at different tables. There are lots of students, and I can't go and talk to all of them every day. I can make my rounds for a whole week, probably, in every class. I go and sit there and do their same project. That way, I can be at their level, and they see what I want from the project.

Denise said that it was especially important to keep learning in science because there are always new discoveries that can even make information in the textbook incorrect.

> There are so many things. It is not like math. Maybe I would feel that way—or maybe, even in English; in science, there are always new developments. My goodness, they have discovered new planets since I have been out of college. I mean, so many things are changing that I have to stay up with it.

It may take a few years for a teacher to feel comfortable with the subject matter, especially if her environment isn't stable. Denise's early teaching experience had been as a traveling teacher, and as such, it was difficult for her to settle into a routine.

> It took maybe two years or so to feel comfortable with the subject matter. It definitely took staying in the same classroom to be able to establish that routine. Being a traveling teacher was not conducive to establishing a productive routine in the classroom and getting everything done, that is for sure…having procedures in place, and that kind of thing.

Jesse has known from an early age that he could teach things well to others:

> I don't know. When I was in elementary, I would strive to do the hard questions so I could explain them to the class. And whenever I would answer stuff that even the teacher had a hard time answering, it showed me that I would be a good person to be a teacher. People would come to me so I could teach them how to do things. I didn't necessarily say, "I am going to be a teacher when I grow up." The reason I went into teaching is because I knew that I was good at it, or I felt I was good at it.

Anabel, the principal of the Newcomer Academy, spoke of a favorite teacher she had, one who opened windows for her. She thought that she would write for the *National Geographic* or for magazines, as he did, because he inspired her so much.

> I can tell you that a day doesn't go by that I don't use something he taught me in that class. If you were to talk to anybody who had the teacher during that time, they would tell you that he was the most popular teacher—but it was hard work. Sometimes, teachers don't know what they do day after day. And I am sure it was hard work for him, although he seemed to have such a great time doing it. His teaching was contagious.

## The Need to Communicate Effectively

One aspect all of the teachers shared in their classrooms was an innate ability to communicate with the students and keep class interesting. Jennifer blended and mixed art and language in her instructions. The warm-up would be a combination of graphics and language. Her classroom was a natural blend of language and art, to support communication. She used simple language that demonstrated to the students what she meant. She took a paper towel, added water, and said, "Class, little water." Then she squeezed the paper towel into the trash to show what a mess a lot of water made. "Little water." They understood her, and her instructions did not interrupt the mood in her class because she continued in a manner that was not disruptive. The students looked up, understood, and kept working. There was a comfortable working environment in the class, and the way she communicated made the class flow smoothly.

Denise displayed charts and graphic organizers for comparison and contrast to support her instruction and communication. Students in her class worked on comparisons and contrasts between complex concepts. They defined jobs and then determined which job was better for them based on certain criteria that had been predetermined. Other students jotted down the procedures of an experiment and worked through the process of the science project.

Denise commented that one thing she learned after years of teaching was that the students did not all have to do the same thing at the same time. This flexibility added an air of momentum to her classroom as students went about the room working on their projects at their own pace. Students who were not as advanced as others did not have a sense of not being able to perform. The manner in which she divided the students also facilitated their effectiveness. She had some mixed groupings, so that the more advanced students could facilitate the learning of the students whose English or knowledge of science was not as secure. A teacher in another class described one of the students Denise chose as a leader as a problem student. Denise put this student in charge of assisting the new Myanmar refugee students who did not know English very well. This responsibility brought out a leadership quality and maturity in the student that was not evident in her other classes.

Melissa used art on her board as a way to work with complex ideas and symbolize how the students could expand their paragraphs. Then she sat down among the groups, engaged the students by looking at their paragraphs again, and explained in more detail what they were working on. Just as the art and science teachers did, Melissa worked closely with the students by circulating in the classroom and using graphics to convey complex issues in a simple way.

Jesse also used graphic explanations often in his math class. The students understood best when they could visualize a problem. Further, he showed that he needed to raise the students' awareness so they could take ownership of their learning. Jesse showed that he, as did the other teachers, employed elements of a cultural and linguistic awareness in his teaching to facilitate communication and make learning interesting.

## Second Language Needs

Language learning can be a barrier for students as they study the subject matter. It can also create a barrier for teachers in becoming close to their students. "Sometimes I feel I can't go to that deep a level with art because of the language barrier," said Jennifer, the art teacher. "I can't take them where I want them to go. That's frustrating sometimes."

Because time was so short, Anabel suggested that one way to facilitate the language learning would be for every teacher to become a language or reading teacher:

> I totally believe in interdisciplinary teaching. I think everyone should be an English teacher. And so, the English teachers should also support thematically what everybody else is doing. Reading has to be the most important class ever, even though it's an elective. Without being literate, the students are not going to be able to hit it. There is an urgency to teach reading.

The language learning needs of students in content area classes were especially challenging. Michael, a social studies teacher, adapted materials and strategies to reach his students. From his interest in developing relationships with the students, he understood that he had to be part language teacher and part social studies teacher. He worked to adapt his material so that the students could understand him. He created these adaptations from his attunement with the students' needs.

When academic adjustments are made, the emotional needs of the students are often met as well because students come to school to learn. When those needs are met by a teacher who sometimes bends over backwards, then the student is touched. This is the kind of behavior that enhances the relationships.

Repeatedly, when asked about the importance of the Newcomer Academy, students told me that it was the understanding nature of the teachers and the importance of learning English that made the school special. Jon came from Pakistan with credits to enter the 10th grade, but he and his family felt that it would take time to learn English solidly and make the transition to the new culture and school system.

> The first year, the teachers were easier than at the regular high school, which helped us a lot. I learned a lot. I was okay, even though most of the students were from Mexico. They were new to the country, too. We had to take the standardized test our junior year. I passed all of my tests and got commended on my social studies. I got better on U.S. history than I did on math. That's funny!

Language learning is important, but it's not an end in itself. Students need to learn English so that they can function in their new school setting.

## Cultural Differences

At the Newcomer Academy, many of the students were from homes of low socio-economic status and the Latino culture. The students created informal cohort groups, which helped them support each other in their transition to the United States. Many of the students had to adjust to both the culture of the United States and the expectations of the schools in this country. The students had to adjust to the U.S. teachers, who were in some ways freer, but on the other hand expected high performance, given the language barriers of these students. In addition, the students who were in a minority, often from Africa or Asia, had a need to be accepted by the majority of students (from Mexico or Central America).

All of the students faced the challenge to grow, respect each other, and interact in spite of the language and cultural differences. A teacher could facilitate this development as well. Jesse mentioned an incident with a boy from the Congo, who was trying to be accepted by some Latina girls. He played a little roughly and teased the students. Unfortunately, they did not understand his roughness, even though he used it in an effort to start friendships. Jesse tried to break through the language barrier and let the student know that he needed to change. It was ironic that the students who might have felt excluded were the ones who had to make the extra effort—or behave in a way that showed maturity—in order to connect with someone in the majority, moving past an injury of exclusion in order to make friends.

> Today there was an incident with Tommie. He doesn't speak Spanish, but I got through to him because he likes to play around very much. He used to pick on students, but when they would pick on him, he would cry; or he

would be like, "They are saying things in Spanish, and I don't understand what they are saying." The same thing happened today. Tommie told this girl something, and she told him, "Callete," be quiet, in Spanish. And he told her, "No, tu callete," because he is learning some Spanish. He grabbed her from the back of the neck; as she was walking out, he pulled her back. So, she turned around and—Boom!—shoves him down.

He freaks out because a girl actually pushed him to the ground. He was on the ground, and she says, "You don't talk to me like that," and da-da-da.

And he looked at me and said, "She pushed me!"

I said, "Well, you started it, so don't come crying to me because I have told you before to respect people if you want to be respected."

So, he started throwing a fit. And Ta Pei, a Taiwanese student, came and told him, "You know what? Teacher told you not to touch other students." He said, "You did it, and now he can't do nothing."

He stood up and said, "It is my bad."

He thinks he is playing. But he is just a rough boy. I got to him. He was about to be mad at me, but he realized that he was the one that messed up.

Jesse helped Tommie move past a cultural barrier by recognizing it and talking with him about it.

*The key you held*
*unlocked a hidden door . . .*
—Barbara McKinley, *Dear Muse* (1995, p. 18)

# 10

## *The Practice of Advocacy*

### *Teachers Working as a Team*

**with Melissa Arasin, Jerry De la Huerta,
Robert Hillhouse, and Denise Norris, Actual Names[1]**

*We want a workplace where employees know they are personally important to us and where they feel comfortable sharing their ideas. And an environment where everyone's ideas are heard. An environment of trust, that allows for personalization of style, where people choose to help. Where they feel compelled to help because they know that we are all responsible for the success of this business. A true team—sharing the pain as well as the gain. We all know how employees can make a difference. They need to know that too.*

—Laurette Koellner (2002)

## Introduction

The literature has placed a great deal of emphasis on the importance of professional learning communities (Blankstein, Houston, & Cole, 2008; Crowther, Ferguson, & Hann, 2008; Hord, 2004), in which teachers continue to learn and work collaboratively (Katzenbach & Smith, 2003). Although the discussion is ongoing in theory, the implementation and practice vary with the ability of the school leadership to adjust schedules, allow for common planning times and common students, and share and distribute power effectively (Sergiovanni, 2007; Spillane & Diamond, 2007a).

The following chapter contains a conversation with one of the three teams of teachers at the Newcomer Academy. This team, the Scorpions, was a group of seven teachers who met together each Tuesday and Thursday during their planning time. On Tuesdays, they met to discuss student issues and outcomes; on Thursdays, they met with the principal for professional development. The teachers viewed the team as a support both for students and themselves. New teachers raised a number of questions during these sessions and also had contact with their teammates during informal conversations in the hallway or between classes. Their ongoing professional development occurred during the entire school year on Thursdays and at other times throughout the year, when outside consultants and professionals came to the school.

## Conversation with the Scorpions

**JB:** Today we're in the science classroom for the team meeting of the Scorpions at the Newcomer Academy. We're going to talk about relationships and their importance in a school setting. The first question I want to ask is: Are relationships with students important? Anybody have an idea on that? You wanted to say something, Denise?

**Denise:** I think relationships between teachers and students are incredibly important; they're the basis for all learning. Before we can engage the students, we have to have some kind of a positive relationship with them.

**Jerry:** Another thing I see with relations is that there has to be respect between both the student and teacher. If there isn't respect, the students will not respect the teacher during class, and learning won't take place.

**JB:** What do you mean by respect?

**Jerry:** Respect: Treat me the way you want to be treated.

**Rob:** Responding to your comment on respect, Jerry, I think that sometimes it seems like students aren't giving the degree of respect that we want. But I think that in those situations, sometimes students can be giving us as much respect as they give to any other adult in their life, or so their parents say at conferences. So, I feel to a certain extent that respect is something we model at this school.

**JB:** You begin the relationship with your students by modeling respect?

**Rob:** I think it's an important part of the relationship.

**JB:** Are relationships as important as the content or information students need to learn? I mean, how important are relationships? Melissa?

**Melissa:** I think they are almost as important. I wouldn't say that it's on the same level, but it is pretty close. I think if there's a negative relationship, students get so preoccupied with it that they shut their ears and eyes to the content. So, if there is a negative relationship, it can overpower the content. If there's a positive relationship, I guess we are bringing the students to a place where they want to learn from us; they are not so preoccupied with hating us, playing tricks on us, and seeing what they can get away with. So relationships are almost as important.

**Cristal:** Like Melissa said, I think relationships are maybe not as important as the content; but they are important, right up there—because if we don't have the relationship, the student will shut down. The relationship allows us to see when a student is shutting down, maybe from another class, or to see if they are having a bad day. We can kind of go to them, not directly, maybe, but kind of, "Hey, are you okay? Are you doing okay today?" Or, "You look kind of sad. You have been kind of quiet." It gives us a chance to open the door.

**Denise:** I actually think the relationships are more important than the content. I have even put more emphasis on them because basically, if the students do not show up to our class and are not engaged, they can't learn anything—or they learn very little. I do take the initiative, as well as I can determine. The students may not think that I have, but I do take the initiative to welcome all students, shake their hand, and say, "Where are you from? I am from here. My name is this. Where are you from?" That kind of thing: "What do you want to be called?" and just come up with something that we share that is special between the two of us.

**Jerry:** I want to say that I think relationships are maybe a little more important than content, especially here at this school. At other schools, I would think that content is more important; but at this school, relationships are a little bit more important, so the students will want to learn in our class. If we have that good relationship with our students in class, they are not going to be afraid of us; they are going to want to talk to us, ask questions, or want to discuss topics in class.

**JB:** Why this school more than other schools?

**Jerry:** Why this school? Because these students have only been here in the United States for two years or less. They feel lost, you know. They are in a place where they don't know anybody, they don't know the area, and they don't know the language. If they talk with people on the street, they don't understand what they are saying. So, we need to have a good relationship because if not, we're going to scare them off. They won't want to come back to school; they won't want to learn.

**JB:** What happens when they return to their neighborhood school—after the two years here at the Newcomer Academy?

**Jerry:** At this school, they start building confidence. They can feel confident about themselves and start learning the language, so they won't feel lost.

**Rob:** As a person who doesn't speak Spanish at all, really, I feel I have to take the initiative with students, particularly with the students that don't have any English or are too scared to start communicating in English. Because my issue is, how do I quickly form a relationship with students when their languages are different? I try to do that through body language and non-verbal interaction, and also, I think, humor, which is kind of universal. Once that has been established, then we can start taking it to the next level, or taking it to other places. My first year at this school, one of the things I found very difficult was comparing myself to teachers who had tremendous relationships with their students. And I felt that—I didn't start having relationships with my students until the second semester in my first year.

**JB:** Why does it take that long?

**Rob:** I think that was when some of the students started to have enough English, and we could start talking. I had asked their math teacher, "Why is it that you have these great relationships with your students?" Because he does; and you know, I don't. He was brutally honest. He said to me, "You know, it's because people don't know you." That's why I let some of my personality start coming out in different ways.

**JB:** What does that mean? You let your personality come out?

**Rob:** I think, for example, my sense of humor.

**JB:** What you do, who you are?

**Rob:** Yes, my expectations and things that I used to think had to be shared through talking in English. But there are other ways to communicate that without language.

**JB:** Can you give an example of another way?

**Rob:** For example—

*(Laughter)*

**Rob:** Denise has just handed me an artifact that a couple of us are using this year. It's a fragment of a coconut shell. It is called the coco loco. A couple of us use this. It is kind of a good-natured way of communicating to a student, "You know, you are a little bit off the rails. You are a little bit crazy today. Today you get the coco loco." And it's interesting because while it is supposed to be humorous and a really a non-consequential intervention, it does impact behavior. I mean, it's a valid warning. This is a really big signal for some students—if they get the coco loco. They aren't happy about that.

**JB:** It's like a way to give feedback in a humorous way.

**Rob:** Yes.

**JB:** Can we just go on around? Olin, do you have something to say about any of this?

**Olin:** I would like to say that it's important to take initiative, especially with our students, because they are new to the country, and they are probably scared. I think it helps them a lot if we make the initial contact and help them feel more comfortable.

**Jerry:** I want to add to that because it is true that they come from a different country. They don't know what it's like here. If you don't take the initiative, they won't take the initiative to have a relationship with you. At the very least, I think we want to or should get to know our students. We are going to see them every day, or every other day, so we need to get to know them. If you don't take the initiative, they won't. I noticed this when I tried it out for a week or so. No one took the initiative to have a relationship with me. No one took the initiative to talk to me or to discuss things in class. But once I saw their boundaries or how much I could push them—because some of them just needed to get pushed a little bit—I did that.

**Melissa:** I want to add to Denise's comment about what she said earlier, about finding one thing that connects us to the students. I think I try to do that by doing something simple. If a student is not really responding to me, I try to find one thing about him that he told me or that he has written about. Then I'll ask him about it, to show him that I am paying attention. I try to do that as much as possible. I wanted to add to Rob's comment, as well. He said he doesn't know much Spanish, so he felt that was something that was keeping him at first from connecting. I noticed myself that I had learned a little Spanish, but I never spoke it. But just saying "¿Como estás?" to that student who is not answering me when I say, "How are you?" because she has no idea about what I am saying; just that, "¿Como estás?" "Bién." Okay. That's like a little seed.

**JB:** You have made a gesture.

**Melissa:** Yes, it's a gesture. So, if I feel that there is something that is hurting that connection, I need only just throw it out, "¿Como estás?" How are you? I mean, it's just a little something.

**Jerry:** There's one thing I wanted to add on to what Rob had said, also. He mentioned about the math teacher who says, "They don't know you," relationship-wise. I guess I can sort of understand where he's coming from. I can relate a little bit more to these students because I have been through a lot of what they've been through. You know, I've been a migrant worker. I've worked in the fields. I have seen hardship. And I've gone through very difficult times. I've gone through things that they've gone through, so I can relate to them a little bit. I guess that is what the math teacher is saying when he says, "They don't even know you." (Jerry is the math teacher's brother.)

**JB:** You can relate to them without saying anything.

**Brandon:** I think the challenge with developing relationships at this school is that communication a very difficult thing. It's a challenge, especially for those of us who don't speak Spanish. We're not going to be able to say certain things to them because it takes so much energy just for them to find a way to say it. One thing I try to do is to never give up on a conversation because having a conversation, even on a really simple and superficial level is a challenge for both of us, you know? I try to never leave it at a point where neither of us understands. If a student is trying to say something to me, and I don't understand him, I always try to keep pushing that student to say something in a way he can, so that there is some kind of understanding.

**JB:** Or even a smile.

**Olin:** Right.

**JB:** Or, perhaps, eye contact.

**Olin:** I keep it going on—just so the students feel that there is some basis for communication between us.

**JB:** Thank you. Do you have any comments on eye contact or how it plays out in your classroom?

**Melissa:** I always personally try to maintain eye contact with whomever is speaking to me, to show respect. If you are not—if you don't have eye contact with someone, it's almost as though you don't respect them. Not in our part of the hallway, but in another part of the hallway, or walking down the street, if we don't make eye contact with another person, it's like we are not even acknowledging their existence. To me, it's so important to have the eye contact that I make our students who are afraid, or who maybe don't give eye contact because of their cultural background—I will say, "Look at me."

**Rob:** I agree. I think we model eye contact in our classrooms. I know that some things can be different from culture to culture. We have so many cultures in our school, so the cultural rules are going to be different. I think we all try to model some kind of eye contact in our classrooms. The one specific moment where I absolutely insist on eye contact is when I am talking with a student, and I need to give a reality check to that student. Maybe there is something I am communicating to him, something important about rules or about something that they need to work on. Oftentimes, in that situation, the student will just drift off, or his head will go wandering around because he doesn't want to hear it. That is the moment where I like to say, "Well, in this culture, you need to actively listen, not just listen with your eyes; but listen with your ears, as well." And especially, in a moment like that, I insist on their making eye contact.

**Cristal:** Yes, I think it is cultural, if they may not look at us, or they kind of look at me and kind of look away. Of course, when it is a reality check, there has to be eye contact. I can tell if a student is kind of listening to me by the eye contact that she makes or not; or if she is just blowing me off through the lack of eye contact. Another thing that is important is our presence in the classroom. It is crucial. We, as teachers, need to be here as much as possible. I try to never be absent from the classroom because the students do see that. And they don't like it. They won't tell us, but they don't like it.

**Denise:** Sometimes they will tell us!

**Cristal:** Yes, and that is another thing about this school. We keep it real, or I keep it real. I think—or they have told me—that they like to be told things as they are. Don't sugarcoat it. Just tell me the way it is. Get to the nitty-gritty, and get it over with. I mean, it works for me.

**JB:** How do you help each other as a team to learn about relationship building?

**Olin:** One thing I would like to say—I think that communication about the background of students helps a lot. For example, if one teacher knows something about a student, like, "Well, so-and-so is kind of off today," then another teacher can say, "Oh, yes. So-and-so had something at home happen." I think that information sharing helps a lot with our team.

**JB:** Do you share information in the hall, or at your team meeting?

**Olin:** More in our team meetings. In the halls, we're pretty busy. We don't have too much time to talk. My team isn't really close to my classroom, or it's not right next door to me. They're down the hall.

**Melissa:** I would say that it helps a great deal because not only can we find out that background information, but also, "How is this student doing in your class? Because, in my class, he is not doing anything, or he's really hesitant." And then you hear, "Well, he's doing okay in my class." So I question, what am I doing wrong? And usually, we can get that help from each other, you know. My classroom is close to both Brandon and Jerry, and a little close to Cristal. I talk to them in the hallway all the time. You know, "What's going on today?" We are next to each other, so we can talk. But then in our team meetings, we all also talk.

**Jerry:** Well, it's true what you say. In our team, we find out what is working in our class and what is not working. Why is he learning in your class, and why can't he learn in my class? What do you do that's so different? But also, as a coach, I know that teamwork is very important. You know, we are a team of seven, not a team of one. That's very important, especially here in this school. We know that we need to have everybody together. And to tell the truth, I've not seen, in any other school that I have visited or worked with, a staff as close as this one. It's very important to work together, to share ideas and strategies, and just to get to know each other. It's the same thing with the student-teacher relation, you know; the student and teacher have the relationship.

**JB:** You are modeling it by working together?

**Jerry:** Yes.

**Denise:** One other thing I wanted to mention is that not only within this team do we work together, but really, among the entire staff and faculty. To give you an example, the other day in science class, we were doing an activity; and one of the math teachers, who is not on our team, happened to be walking by. And he saw all the equipment we had out, and he was interested in it. So he came in to see what we were doing and play with the equipment. And in the process, I made the comment, "Well, these particular students"—they were some new students that came from Burma—"they don't know how to do this activity; they don't understand how to do a graph. They don't know graphing." "Oh, I taught them that today!" So, he went over to the new students: "Pull out your paper from my class today." So, they pulled out their paper. And lo and behold, it was pretty much the same thing. And so the students had an "ah-ha!" moment. They were like, "Oh, this is what you want us to do." So then, they understood. The math teacher stood there and played a little bit with our equipment while they did the work. It made a big difference in the kind of output we got from those students, as far as that particular assignment.

**JB:** Working collaboratively during class time seems to be a big help with that last example. I'm going to transition to another topic. Did any of you get staff development at this school, or training in multicultural education in your teacher-training program about how to work with multi-culturally diverse students?

**Rob:** I think we have lived this kind of training at this school. I can't remember having training sessions on multicultural-ism. And I can't imagine why not, because we get students from unusual parts of the world. Maybe the time for us to discuss that kind of thing is in a group, actually. I think we are culturally sensitive a lot. Sometimes I wish that we had some training because I can think of cultural misunderstand-ings that happened in my class in the last couple of years, the most egregious one being the conflict between my cultures—because I really don't know what a regular American high school classroom looks like; I know what a British classroom looks like—so there is a culture clash for everyone, straight-away (Rob is from Scotland). But I had a culture clash with one student from Sudan when he first arrived. He was quite uncomfortable in my classroom. So, yes, I wish I could be more culturally sensitive with a couple of students because I feel that when we start off on the wrong foot, it takes a long time to recover.

**Denise:** When I was an undergraduate, we had a little bit of train-ing in multi-culturalism, but it pretty much focused on the Spanish-speaking countries; it was not very useful in our situa-tion at all.

**JB:** Would it have been something you could have used?

**Denise:** It could have been if it had included more things like Rob was mentioning about the cultures that we see reflected in our student body.

**JB:** What about language training, such as SIOP? Is that a help? Are you able to adapt, not just from the language point of view, but perhaps from a relationship point of view? Is it some-thing you can apply immediately? (Sheltered Instructional Observational Protocol [SIOP] is a method of sheltered Eng-lish used for second language learners in academic settings).

**Melissa:** I just had the SIOP training last week. That was my first time to be really introduced to it. We had been kind of gathering this information through different trainings with groups such as West Ed, DL, a little bit, I guess. But we need to supple-ment that; we can't just hand them something and expect them to get it. We have to supplement and add a few other things—to scaffold, or use pictures, visuals—especially with

SIOP. That training was helpful to me because it showed me new ways to give them more language, like vocabulary words. The students need to make associations and not just have a definition. Give an example. Draw a picture. What are some synonyms? You know? I think those things are very helpful, especially as a first-year teacher and a first-year sheltered instruction teacher.

**JB:** Is SIOP something you are able to do in the other content areas, or is it easier in English?

**Rob:** SIOP is like when you have—and Denise can correct me, if my biology is off—if I have two trees, and I graft part of the second tree onto the first tree, well, now I have a modified the first tree because of this graft. I view SIOP as being like that: The tree is the teacher, and SIOP is the graft. Regardless of the content area, the SIOP graft allows each teacher to have some basics of language acquisition grafted onto him or her. Sometimes, that graft will work better than other things. That could be due to a variety of factors. But what I want to argue is that, while we have a great relationship with SIOP in our school, and while we have had just incredible support from SIOP, and while SIOP is very valid, including the content and language objectives, for us, we are kind of beyond grafting. We are interested, if I can continue the tree analogy, in creating true hybrids in the laboratory. SIOP is a good start, but it doesn't provide specifics, and it doesn't look at things on the level of task selection, flow, or give specific types of scaffolding or curricular overview. In other words, for us, its utility is limited.

**JB:** You are beyond that? Is that what you are saying?

**Rob:** We are a bit beyond that. SIOP works as a baseline, but SIOP is what every student has to do as a language learner in a class. We are beyond that just by the nature of the beast. It is fair to say that is why we are pursuing other things, such as Differentiated Learning, from the University of Pittsburgh and Quality Learning (Q-Tel) from West Ed.[2]

**JB:** In an ideal world, what would you want to add or change with your program here?

**Cristal:** More time. You could just work here 24/7, 365 days a year, and you still would not be done.

**JB:** Why does it take so long?

**Cristal:** It just takes time. And I think the students are already limited, or they come to us late. We just have this little bit of time— two years, or one year, or whatever—to teach them everything that a native student has been learning through nine or ten years of schooling. So, just more time.

**JB:** Would you like a four-year program?

**Cristal:** That is a possibility. But at the same time, as a teacher, we could immerse ourselves in being a teacher 24/7, 365, and we still wouldn't get it all done. We could draw the line and say, "Okay, I am out of here at 3:45," but are we really productive or effective if we do that?

**Brandon:** First of all, in an ideal world, I think some of our students probably need more time. Secondly, I think it would be great for our students to have more opportunities to advance or develop their own language. And I think, thirdly, that a lot, if not most of our students need some kind of opportunity, at least part of the day or class, where they are specifically just learning language, kind of like an ESL-type of class.

**JB:** Would you want to see this program connected or become a conduit to a community college? Where maybe the students spend three or four years here and then go into a vocational or academic program at a community college?[3]

**Melissa:** I am not really answering your question. I am kind of answering it. I think that they need real-world experience, some kind of exposure to native speakers. We went to the next town and visited Aquarena Springs, but how much did they have to communicate with people outside of the students and faculty? I think that they just need to go out and talk to people.

**JB:** In the community.

**Melissa:** In the real world, because we are kind of in a bubble here. I am afraid that when they do go out, if they try to be the same way with their new teachers as with us, that they are going to get shut down. Maybe that person won't be as receptive or understanding. But also, they need to know how to go to a grocery store and what to say to a cashier. I don't know if they are doing these things. I really don't know how we could do that.

**Rob:** The change that I want in comparison to these global aims is so selfish. Instead of having textbooks, the change I would like is to have a class set of laptops. I teach geography this year. I have so many geography materials, textbooks, auxiliaries to textbooks ... I have a giant bookshelf filled with all of these "official" resources adopted by the school district. Not only is the textbook unfit for students in many ways, it is also, in some places, actually culturally offensive. So even if the students could access the textbook, and it was not out of their reach, I don't know if I would even give it to them.

*My idea,*
*not judged*
*but listened to*
*with a light continuance.*

*The idea poised—*
*materializing*
*at any moment,*
*inspired.*

—Barbara McKinley, *Dear Muse* (1995, p. 23)

# 11

## *The Practice of Advocacy*

### *The Role of Leadership*

*As far as we can discern, the sole purpose of human existence
is to kindle a light in the darkness of mere being.*

—Carl Jung (1962, p. 326)

## The Role of Leadership in Advocacy

A building leader and district supports are critical in establishing new structures of accommodations. The Newcomer Academy was conceived of and developed at the district level, and the building leader was given broad leeway, funding, and support to accomplish the school's goals. The leader had to deal with constraints such as class size and meeting times. The principal set the tone for the faculty and staff. By meeting the personal needs of the adults in the building (the need to advance, feel valued, be heard, and so on), the principal showed that these same concerns from the students would also be respected. The necessity for teachers to accommodate the ac-

*Care & Advocacy: Narratives from a School for Immigrant Youth,* pages 133–143
Copyright © 2012 by Information Age Publishing

ademic needs of the students was another issue for the principal to address. Ongoing professional development of multiple types: specialized training in sheltered English for all teachers, training in how to cover essential topics for the standardized tests, and how to give the teachers the structure for this work on an ongoing basis were critical challenges to face.

In addition to the academic support, the personal, social, and emotional needs of the staff and students were foremost. In the Newcomer Academy, the social worker—one for 300 students—was given a central voice. She was allowed to interrupt classes to call students for hearing and sight tests and dental exams. Awareness of health needs was a priority, and every advisory teacher worked to make sure that the students knew where to get their vaccinations. The counselor also worked through the advisory system—one for 300 students. All of the students went over their plan of study, knew the college requirements, and listened to representatives from colleges when they came to speak. The advisory system, along with the team structure, created a means for communicating in the school and for the teachers to act collaboratively on behalf of the students.

## Working within Constraints

The teachers and, to some extent, the students, discussed barriers to practicing *care* or developing caring relationships in the classroom. Those in staff positions sometimes said that they were able to relate to students in ways in which teachers could not, implying that they could be with the students as individuals and without the constraints of classroom management. In addition, because the staff was Latino, the implication was that staff members spoke the language of the majority of the students and in that way moved past the barriers with students. Classroom practices that were discussed included time, class size, language learning issues, cultural differences, and the tone in the classroom.

### Time

Several concerns arise in regard to time and the immigrant adolescent population. The first concern is that it takes time to learn English. Adolescents who come to the United States have high expectations placed upon them, and graduating in four years from a high school can be a stumbling block because of the demands placed upon the students for performance. Placing realistic expectations on a student and understanding the time line for achievement is a *caring* topic when we consider that aspects of *care* include the abilities to be attuned with the students, attend to their needs, and make adjustments. During a team meeting, Melissa, the English teacher put the issue of time this way:

> Aside from the normal constraints in the school day for teachers, adolescent immigrant students are under time constraints to learn a new language as fast as they can. Everyone involved with this population says that the adolescent immigrant students have no time for anything extra.

Anabel, the principal, said:

> We have to make every minute count. This is a two-year program in which we have to get the students up to speed and ready for their neighborhood schools. We have two years to make up so much, so every second, every moment, is a teachable moment. That is our task right now—the sense of urgency is high.

Another time consideration for the Newcomer Academy students included the travel time they spent on the buses every day. This school was a two year pullout program, and students took from one to three school buses to make the drive across town to the Academy. This meant at least an hour each way, morning and night. They left their houses at 7:00 a.m. and got home around 6:00 or 7:00 in the evening. The students, then, had very little time to do homework or participate in extracurricular activities because of their extensive commute time. Melissa, the English teacher, said:

> They are getting up at the crack of dawn to get here because they have to ride two or three buses. And then they do not get home until late. It (was like) my (high school) life, but I think it is much harder for them because they don't speak English. It is hard. I hope that at some point in the future, I can look back and say, "Okay, I did meet the students' needs, when it comes to academics."

One positive aspect of the bus rides is that the students created relationships with others and experienced the transition together. Although it took time away from learning, the time was given over to a group who shared experiences in adjusting to a new school system and new country together. Many students talked about how the bus rides were fun because they talked with their friends. In summary, everyone shared a sense of urgency with regard to what the students must accomplish in so short a time.

### *Class Size*

At times teachers would talk about the size of the classes. It is true that English as a Second Language (ESL) classes were often smaller in size, ranging from 15 to 20 students per class. It is demanding to teach large classes when many students do not know the language. When students all come from one language group, then a teacher can give instructions in their native language if she knows it. When the groupings of students are mixed, teachers must know ESL teaching strategies. Large classes make it difficult to always be sure that all of the students' basic language and emotional needs are being met. A dialogue with Jennifer, the art teacher, about class size:

> **JB:** How many students do you teach during the day?
>
> **Jennifer:** Today I just had 120.
>
> **JB:** Is that how many you have in all?
>
> **Jennifer:** That is total.
>
> **JB:** How do you handle all those students? Do you ever feel that there are too many demands placed on you to care about the students as individuals?
>
> **Jennifer:** I have it kind of nice. Other classes have 30 or more.
>
> **JB:** How many are in each class that you have?
>
> **Jennifer:** My highest is 25. That class is a little crazier; it is harder to get stuff done. But once it gets going, it is the same thing with every class.

When classes are large, it is hard for teachers to develop solid relationships with each student, especially when language-learning issues are present.

## Taking Care of Teachers' Personal Needs

The principal made sure that teachers felt valued. She supported those who wanted to advance, helped teachers feel valued, and recognized their need to be heard by being generous with her time to listen.

### *Need to Advance*

Anabel, the principal, let me leave early on Tuesdays to attend classes. She encouraged a math teacher to enter the principalship program and, in general, recognized that teachers needed to advance:

I think that it's important to support people and their growth. You can't have a dream that is unreal—that people will stay with you forever. But you can develop a system where they hand off to the next person, and the expectations are in place. So, what I do for people is show them that they have a lot of potential to grow, and I support them in that growth. Some people want to go to classes at the university, some people want to serve on committees, or some people want to be part of the leadership or curriculum team. Whatever it is that they want to do, I encourage them to do it. In fact, I expect them to do something because a stagnant person, well, that is all they can produce: stagnant and boring instruction. We have to be lifelong learners in order to best know our core content and understand how we are going to deliver it. If I support people in what they need to do, they will be better with kids.

It is an enthusiasm for learning that is just contagious. If the teachers are doing it, their students must also. And then we have a healthy competition going, you know, with "My student can do better than your student," and that is just healthy. It isn't promoting any kind of competition that is detrimental to the academic progress of the kid, the teacher, or the principal. First and foremost, I have to support people in what they need to do, and they will be better with kids.

### Need to Feel Valued

Teachers felt so valued that they didn't want to stay without their principal. One particular teacher was allowed to pick up her daughter from day care during her planning period and keep her at school for the last class. Not every child could have done so, but the principal knew that this teacher and her child would succeed with this plan. Not many principals would have allowed such a bending of the rules, but this kind of advocacy set the tone for the school. Jennifer, the art teacher, explained:

> I mean, I told Anabel that if she ever quits being a principal, I am going to quit being an art teacher. Because I really do feel a lot of support from them, in the sense—Because, I mean, what goes on in art class goes on in the student's life . . . I don't feel any kind of pressure.

Asked how she thinks the students feel about the class, and if she though they would say they enjoyed it:

> Yes. I think they just feel good here. I think this class is a safe place. They get to socialize a little, and they get to be creative and use the side of their brain that they don't get to use most of the day.

When Jennifer was asked, "Would you say that you touch the students in a deep way? " she said, "I think so... I think it takes them the full year, though."

### Need to Be Heard

The principal told stories of her own adolescence and revealed that she had an inclination for seeing people's needs or personal dilemmas:

> I didn't want to be a teacher. Actually, I got involved in the school newspaper. I found out that I was a pretty good writer. Freshmen could not be on the newspaper staff, and I really wanted to be. I found a student who really did not want to be in that class, and I said, "Let me write your stuff for you. Let me do it, and then you turn it in and see what the teacher says."

> We did this the whole year, and my work would be published. One of the articles was about one of our custodians. I had watched him every day. He seemed to be preoccupied with something, and this job was just a job. So, I started talking to him and found out that he had been a bullfighter. He had been a bullfighter in Mexico, and he even had posters of himself as a bullfighter. And now he has come to the United States, and he is a custodian. How do you go from the middle of an arena fighting bulls to cleaning the cafeteria? I put a positive spin on it, you know; then I wrote a feature story on this man and turned it in...

## Taking Care of Teachers' Academic Needs

The teachers needed support in working with second language learners. Many of the teachers had just graduated from the university, and some didn't even have their English as a Second Language endorsement. Teachers were given a structure for professional development every Thursday during their planning time and had a lateral team meeting with the same group of teachers every Tuesday. The teams were mixtures of veteran and new teachers, so they also provided support among themselves in their discussions.

### Ongoing Professional Development

Anabel described the professional development in place at the school:

> We just had a PLC (Professional Learning Community) last Thursday where we laid out what was important to us. I can't tell you everything we will do this year, but we do have the big pieces of it. What is important to us, of course, is that we care for our kids and our students' welfare. We want the

students to be able to pass a test that will determine whether or not they will be successful in high school. Therefore, we must teach the essential skills, or TEKS, in order for them to pass the state-mandated tests in the subject areas, or TAKS test. We are involved with the Institute for Learning with the Disciplinary Literacy.

The Institute for Learning is out of the University of Pittsburgh. They help us teach the content areas with rigor. We focus on the essential skills that will actually be tested. Additionally, we work with a group from San Antonio, IDRE, to provide SIOP (Sheltered Instructional Observational Protocol). To follow up on this training, we have ongoing training with West Ed under Alda Walqui. Their program is called Quality Teaching; it helps teachers learn from each other how to adapt the material in a consistent manner throughout the school and develop pedagogical strategies that support that rich, higher level questioning to take students to a deeper level of thinking. The Dana Center is helping us with math. We're looking at how all of these programs will fit together to support our efforts.

The different teams were divided, and within these teams, the teachers discussed what we would like. Next Thursday, we will whittle it to what this can look like in the school year. This will be the foundation for their professional development planning the rest of the year. Where are we weak? What do we need more work in? What do we need to look at? Do we know the test? Are we aligning our classes with the TEKS and basing the classes on the test? We don't know the tests very well, so we have to focus on them in the upcoming year so that our lessons are really on target. We are evaluating our own assessments and sharing the work with each other. We have very defined tools that we are using across the board to deliver that instruction.

In addition to receiving training on how to teach, the teachers also meet by discipline and observe each other's classes. Anabel said:

The department meetings are every other Thursday after school, every other week, and also on a late start day. We have late start days that are dedicated to their core subject area. We also visit each other on something called learning walks. At first teachers were hesitant to do this because it was hard to talk about their own teaching. One team would go visit another team, and then they came back and debriefed about what they saw. It was easier to talk about another team than to talk about themselves.

Then I hired a substitute teacher so that they could go to the classrooms of teachers with students that they all shared. They could see their students in classes with other teachers and see how other teachers handled the students and their subject matter.

## *Providing Resources*

Providing resources to support the teachers was also important. The school made a substantial financial commitment to professional development efforts with multiple consultants. In addition, the principal liked to provide curricular resources for the teachers to use in their classrooms. She instructed the support staff that when a teacher needed something—some use of their time for their classroom—it would be a priority:

> I have always told the support team or staff, the teachers are the front line. We are almost the sacrificial lambs for the cause because we have to make sure that the teachers have everything they need. They are the front line that connects with the kids. But I expect the support team to do that, be friendly, and be customer—you know, service-oriented, and all. That is a lot of pressure on some people.
>
> They are also included in the training so that they understand the goals of our program. Everybody is included in the goals of the program. Everyone knows the goal. When someone comes in and says, "I need this right now," it is hard to always remember that. Knowing the goals of our program helps keep that focus.

## *Providing a Structure for Collaboration*

Such collaboration can take place because the teachers are organized into three teams with common students of about 100 each. This arrangement allows the teachers to talk about student issues on Tuesdays during their planning times, and to discuss professional development on Thursdays with the principal or an outside consultant. Anabel said:

> As this school has developed, more and more conversation is strictly about instruction. This year, we are even cutting out our school-wide faculty meetings; we don't have any of those anymore. We are constantly talking to each other, so we don't need faculty meetings. If I have anything to say, I may send it out in an e-mail. If we need to come together as a group, then we will, to deal with something that is out of the content area, academics. I might call an important meeting if a vote is necessary, but for the most part, faculty meetings are out. Team meetings are in, and the faculty comes together all by themselves.
>
> A team is made up of at least five of the content area teachers: English, Reading, Math, Science, and Social Studies. And then we tap into the elective teachers that I purposely have off that period, to be part of a team. We have three teams, and all teachers are in one of those three teams. They

meet twice a week: once on Tuesday, or it started out to be—excuse me—discipline and related business. More and more, it is gearing itself up for more academic discussion and for visiting other people's classrooms. And then, Thursday is our professional learning community or PLC meeting in which we come together; and right now, we are developing protocols for what those are going to look like. They will include analyzing data, looking at student work, and analyzing our own assessments and how to push for more progress. How are we going to measure that? And so, those are our Thursday meetings.

A lot of times, the teachers are worn out. So, am I merciful with the PLC time? No, they come dragging in here; they look tired sometimes, but here we are at this PLC. I'm sure someone is thinking, "Frick 'em, frack 'em, frig 'em. You know, if I could just, I would throw a shoe at her." You know? But in the end, you wouldn't give up the camaraderie, the feeling of being united in an academic focus, as well as the welfare of the kids as much as anything. It is just out there because we spend that time together.

The team leader gives me the notes from the Tuesday team meetings, and I read them. From the notes, I can gauge the climate of the faculty: If they want me to know something, or if they want to say, "Your strategy stinks," they can write it in the notes, and I won't know who said it. One of the questions was, "How does Tuesday differ from Thursday?" That was a great question. My interpretation is that if Tuesdays are looking more like Thursdays, then that is awesome. That means there are less discipline and student issues. If they are not talking so much anymore about discipline, it means that they are engaging kids more in the classroom—that's great!

My day is full of figuring out how to pay for things, and how to better serve the teachers in their classrooms. What do they need; what are they looking for? Are there any grants that we can write?

## Teachers in Turn Setting the Tone, Class by Class

The principal talked about her first year of teaching. She drew on her own experiences repeatedly to help develop empathy for her teaching staff. It showed the importance of caring for the teachers because they, in turn, cared for the students. When the students feel cared for, they take care of the school and each other—and even the teacher, when she needs it. Anabel explained:

> With all the experience I have now, I would be a much better teacher today than I was my first year. I remember that in my first year of teaching, my husband passed away at Christmas. I was coming back to work after the holidays. The story of his death had been all over the news because he was a policeman killed on duty. I was a pitiful picture. My son was eight months old, and

here I was, a young woman left with a baby, and all the tragedy…they had the funeral on TV. He was a young policeman, but he had already received a number of commendations—24 commendations. He had been selected as a national peace officer of the year—he had done a lot, even though he was only in his 20s. He was even on national news. And so, yes, the kids heard about it. When I got back to school, I was very, very sad. And it was because of them, I think, that I could even get up in the morning. I can't tell you that I was the best teacher that year. But they were. They were. They were the best teachers. I did not do them justice, but they did it all for me.

They taught me many things that semester about why I could go on, why I needed to go on, why they needed me to go on…There was teaching done on both sides, I guess; but for myself, I learned from them how to get through a crisis, because I knew they cared. I knew they cared about me. They were willing to take care of me that semester, and to make sure that I was at my best; they behaved as well as they possibly could and did whatever else they could for me. Whatever they could, they did.

Even though the professional development had an academic focus, the principal developed the affective domain at the school by the way she treated the staff and students. The teachers and students felt it and responded. Anabel said:

That is a very important part of the whole endeavor—making sure that we have developed relationships with our students. Caring relationships, where we might step out of our teacher roles; and because we are fellow human beings, we will stop to help in whatever way we can. Everyone here does that. Everyone just does that.

When asked if she tries to hire teachers who would have that instinct, Anabel said:

Absolutely. They can see the need of the student coming to them from a mile away, and you know, they are willing to get in there and do something about it and try and help. I do have a lot of people who are willing to do that, a lot of people who look inside a kid.

## Implications for Practice

Experienced teachers tell us that relationships are of primary importance in schools, yet the interpersonal aspects of schooling are often left to develop on their own.

The focus for school improvement is most often on academics, especially with the push towards accountability. We have attempted to move from models of leadership based solely on management and business models to those that embrace the social and cultural context within which our students live.

Caring, and understanding the importance of how to develop relationships with students, peers, staff, administrators, parents, and community members have tremendous potential for motivating students to develop their social, emotional, and personal aspects as well their academics. Students will perform better if given individual attention (see, for example, the website for the Collaborative for Academic, Social, and Emotional Learning, www.casel.org).

## Next Steps

The care ethic has most often been embraced within a curriculum and instruction tradition. Social and emotional development hails from a tradition of psychology and human development. The social work tradition involves families and schools with community services, and the humanities and humanistic traditions have given us a window into the importance of understanding our ethical and moral needs and aspirations. Building schools from these varied strands and disciplines of human development can join to serve children in our schools; collaboration allows these perspectives to be heard together. In the 21st century, this collaborative endeavor can take us to a sense of social and moral justice. Leadership is poised to guide us on this next step of the journey.

> *Through grace we*
> *are saved to*
> *walk on this*
> *scorched earth.*

—Barbara McKinley, *Second Verse* (2003, p. 11)

# Migratory Path of Monarch Butterflies

A friend, Mike Medrano, called it to my attention that monarch butter-flies migrate north throughout the United States each year and then return south to Mexico in the winter months. When they travel back to Mexico, it's hard to pinpoint exactly where they go; in fact, people speak of their home with a sense of reverence. The butterflies travel to a place high in the mountains that cannot be located easily. Locals respect their home as a natural mystery.

I had the map of the migration of the monarchs on my desk, as well as a map of the Hispanic/Latino population in the United States. Something caught my eye as I looked at the maps; there was a good deal of overlap between these two maps.

The similarity would make sense since the butterflies would follow the blossoms of apple, cherry, orange, and peach trees, and patches of grapes, lettuce, artichokes, and other produce to California, the Texas Rio Grande Valley, Oregon, Maine, and elsewhere. Those who immigrate are not solely following the fruits of the earth, but their paths perhaps follow those natural roadmaps, as a way to survive.

*Care & Advocacy: Narratives from a School for Immigrant Youth,* pages 145–146

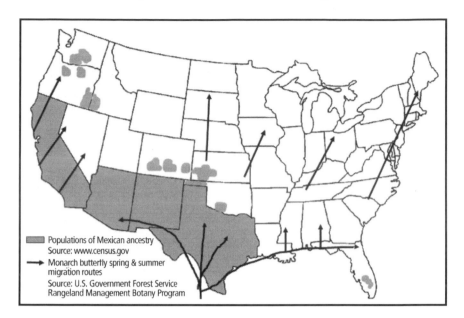

**Figure 1**  This map approximates the overlap of the Mexican population cluster in the South, Southwest, and Western portion of the United States and the migratory paths of the Monarch butterflies.

We humans strive for a better life that exceeds the expectations of nature and beyond the dreams that showed as a gleam in a parent's or grandparent's eye when they followed their dreams.

They say that it might take many generations for the monarchs to make the complete migratory path, just as it might take several generations for an immigrant family's roots to take hold in their new home.

> *What appears and what is, often is not.*
> —Barbara McKinley, *Dear Muse* (1995, p. 36)

APPENDIX **A**

# Researcher's Stance, Ethics, and Narrative Inquiry

*The research on man, the interest of science and society should never take precedence over considerations related to the well-being of the subject . . .*
—United Nations Helsinki Declaration, 1975

## Researcher's Stance

My own experiences as a child, student, parent, and educator have influenced my interpretations and understandings of the researcher's stance, ethics, and choice of narrative inquiry.

I interviewed the students during their fourth year of study in the United States, when those who were in school were seniors. The year they graduated was also the year of my own graduation. These students at the Newcomer Academy represented many nationalities, and they were also survivors. Many of their peers did not remain in school very long after they moved from the two-year transitional Newcomer Academy back to their neighborhood high schools. Some of the students had bounced around among three or four schools before they finally left school forever. Students' names would show up on the monthly school rosters as no-shows, failures, or as having excessive absences. The students on monthly rosters were dropped from the school rolls, so their failure or absence would not adversely affect the Annual Yearly Progress (AYP) report for the school.

I remember asking one of the students, "What happened to Omar? Didn't I see him here earlier this year?"

"Oh, Miss, he only lasted two days."

After they had received intensive support from the school district for their first two years, only handfuls of students graduated from the various neighborhood home schools in what would have been their senior year. In fairness to the schools, this population moved quite a bit, and it is hard to say how much that mobility contributed to this process. One day I received a call from a student.

"Hello, my name is John Lion," he said in English.

It was surprising to hear him speak English to me. After two years of communicating with him between my limited Spanish and his limited English, I savored how freely he spoke with me now. I had always known him as Juan Leon.

"I'm in Dallas now, and I don't know where to go for summer school."

I had given my phone number to all of the students when I left and said, "If you ever need anything, let me know."

John, or Juan, as I had known him, had called me after a year in school in Dallas to help him understand where to go for summer school. "Didn't he know someone there to call? " I thought.

This study is not about one school, but about the complex arrangement called urban schooling. The Newcomer Academy started students on their educational journey in a positive direction, so much so that students experienced and remembered the school in a warm way.

The students had special accommodations for their first two years, and then, unlike many of their peers from the neighborhood home school, they moved past their freshman year and entered their neighborhood schools as juniors. Many of the teachers were not prepared to receive these students, who were still learning English. Even though they could speak social English, the students had many challenges in reading the textbooks, listening in class, taking notes, and responding to teachers' questions.

In Texas, the new immigrants had approximately two years of sheltered support. Some of them entered their classrooms, invisible to the teachers as new immigrants because their peers had immigrated earlier in elementary or junior high school. On other occasions, their peers were children of second or third generation immigrant parents. They blended in, and it is highly likely that their teachers did not have a sense that the Latino/ Hispanic students in their classes had these varied immigration patterns and language abilities. The students blended into the American history, chemistry, and analytical geometry classes among the other 11th graders at the school. Some of them were in advanced placement Spanish classes, as the Newcomer Academy counselor and assistant principal had worked hard to get credits transferred and advanced or pre-advanced placement classes for students whenever possible.

The 11th grade English teachers did not have many English learners at one time; therefore, they had little knowledge and few skills required to accommodate the students' unique needs. The 11th grade American history teachers also struggled to make accommodations for this group. The students did not have dedicated social workers, staff members to greet them in the halls, or teachers who knew how to use sheltered English in their classes. The students were not contained in a small geographic space but instead seemed to get lost in classes found throughout all parts of the large school campus. The students missed the cohort experience during their long bus rides and in the strong peer groups that worked with similar issues.

Watching the students disappear became a concern for me. Because I had been their teacher for two years, the students still viewed me as their teacher. As a result, I had to be especially concerned with ethical considerations when I set up the research. Would they respond to me just because of their respect for me as a teacher? Would they jeopardize their position because of their relationship with me?

One of the students I visited in his neighborhood high school wasn't there the first time I went. I thought, "Well, I'll go to the staff person who helps new immigrant students and see if I can ask her to visit him about college requirements." I went to her, but she didn't know him. I found out later that he had illegally paid to get a green card, or status to be in the United States, and that at the school he was considered a resident. In my attempt to help, I could have caused him problems. A fine line exists between helping and meddling, especially in this case if the student had not asked for help. Because of situations like this, experienced teachers might hesitate to get involved.

Some of the issues I considered were my prior relationships with the students, their vulnerability, the tradeoff between the benefits of the study and risks to the participants, the students' expectations of me, my ability to offer help if needed, and the design of the research itself. In the example above, I had clearly crossed a line. However, in some cases, students did ask for help with large fines or parking tickets, assistance with a paper, or other requests. In conducting laboratory and medical research, such situations repeatedly arise. Ethical considerations are routinely weighed, especially if the researchers are in a position to help the participants as a regular part of their work. Medical researchers have dealt with subtle, ethical issues when conducting research (Riis, 2003; Shamoo & Resnik, 2009; United Nations, 1975).

## Ethical Considerations

Although ethical considerations are important in any study, they are crucial when working with students from vulnerable populations. These considerations are especially important for students with whom a personal relationship has developed.[1]

### *My Prior Relationship with the Students*

Because of my former teacher status with the students I interviewed, I was aware that they held an expectation for me to act as a teacher; that is, they perceived me to be a teacher because that had been my relationship with them. In some sense, it underscores the permanence and power of the role of teacher. Teresa, one of the students who lived in my neighborhood, would bring her young niece by when she visited. Her niece would address me as "mi maestra," or my teacher. Teresa's family members even saw me as a teacher because of my relationship with her. The students trusted that I had their best interests at heart, as any teacher does. They could not separate my role as a teacher who cared about them from my role as a researcher; as such, I honored their notion of who I was at all times. I put considerations for them above the research and confidential information that they shared with me. As a result, these data have not been shared in this report. Further, the students responded and opened up even more fully to my daughter, who helped me serve some of their needs that were exposed in the process of the interviews. Again, because these students confided in her, and not in me, I have not included that information in this study. Although I interviewed them because I found we could speak honestly, I felt that this familiarity created boundaries for me as a researcher; I was honor-bound to protect them.

## Vulnerability of the Subjects

The population studied was vulnerable due to their tentative legal and financial status in the United States, as well as the language barriers, which often resulted in learning difficulties in school. Therefore, it became important for me to realize that my continued relationship as a teacher was vital to them. I was especially sensitive of their vulnerability within their neighborhood high school, where they may not have felt close to teachers or adults or been able to speak openly with them.

My meetings with the students for interviews took on an importance that went beyond the actual interview itself. One of the subjects, Alicia, was a bright young student who had kept up email contact with me when she lived in another city for two years prior to the beginning of the study. She subsequently returned, so I asked her if I could interview her for this project. My interviews with her took many turns, many of which were attributed to her fragile relationship with her father, who was often out of town. Her relationship with her aunt, who lived next door, was also unstable in that she indicated she did not want to take care of Alicia or worry about how she did in school.

As I began to learn the personal details about students in the interview process, I worked to keep a distance. I realized that the students viewed me as an adult who could and perhaps should be responsive. I should be someone who helped, if it were possible. I sometimes took this role, within reason. The notion that somehow I would remain an objective observer was, for me, out of the question. The very fact that I selected these students to be in the research project meant I was no longer objective because I had an established, ongoing relationship with these students. A teacher will evaluate, monitor, advise, propose, encourage, and guide, as well as care. As a researcher, I took a similar stance by donning the persona of a professional who had an obligation to take action, especially when I saw two students' graduation in jeopardy if I did not take that action. I was reminded of Ruth Behar's opening essay of The Vulnerable Observer (1996), in which she explained why a photographer threw his camera aside when he realized that the subject of his photographs was being sucked into the clay to her death:

> In 1985 an avalanche in Colombia buried an entire village in mud. Isabel Allende, watching the tragedy on television, wanted to express the desperation she felt as she helplessly observed so many people being swallowed by the earth. In her short story *Of Clay We Are Created*, Allende writes about Omaira Sanchez, a 13-year-old girl who became the focus of obsessive media attention. News-hungry photographers, journalists, and television camera people, who could do nothing to save the girl's life, descended upon her

as she lay trapped in the mud, fixing their curious and useless eyes on her suffering. Amid that horrid audience of onlookers, which included Allende herself watching the cruel "show" on the screen, she places the photographer Rolf Carle. He, too, has been looking, gazing, reporting, and taking pictures. Then something snaps in him. He can no longer bear to watch silently from behind the camera. He will not document tragedy as an innocent bystander. Crouching down in the mud, Rolf Carle throws aside his camera and flings his arms around Omaira Sanchez as her heart and lungs collapse (1996, p. 1).

With Alicia, who had issues that were keeping her from attending school, my daughter helped show her how she could take care of her staggering traffic fines. Alicia was so devastated by the letter from the court, which she received while her dad was working in the north, that she wouldn't get out of bed. This student transferred her relationship with me to my daughter and, to this day, they stay in touch with each other through email contact and visits.

For me, my role as a researcher has always been secondary to that as an educator. This priority is the nature of my work. When I observe in a classroom and see that a student needs help, that student will still view me as a teacher. As such, I will help him because I regard the needs of that student as greater than my need to record the actions of interest. The student perceives me as someone who can help; but aside from that perception, I also am compelled to do it. After visiting one class a few times, I found myself sitting with a table of refugees from Myanmar. They had only newly been introduced to English, spoke a language with a different sentence structure from English, and were surrounded by Hispanic students who had been in the school for at least six months. I pointed to pictures and helped them develop a simple vocabulary while I was in the classroom.

I ran into one of the refugees from Myanmar in the hallway. She asked me why I wasn't coming back, and I explained that I had just finished visiting. The Myanmar refugees had very limited English and were in classes with predominantly Spanish speakers, so when they needed help, they could turn only to the teacher. In many of these classes with 20 students or more, the teacher was accustomed to the strong students assisting those who needed help. During the few days that I sat at their table, I'd point to the picture, write a word, or give a sample answer that helped the students with enough information to get started. Without someone like me there in the classroom to help, they'd have to wait until the teacher could arrive at their table. Because they sat quietly, the other clamoring, noisy students got to the teacher first. The request from the student broke my heart because I knew how much she needed someone to help.

## Benefits and Risks

When I began to realize that these interviews would take me places I had not anticipated, I found that I carefully had to weigh the risk of my involvement with the benefits of the research. I worked to put the students' pressing personal needs out of my mind, as I knew that all of the students had families, and that I was one person who could only do so much. I had not anticipated finding out so much about their suffering, pending court actions, and dire financial needs. The family strength and bonds were important to the students, whether that family structure was in the United States or elsewhere. Even the memory of a loving family or their presence in other locations was a strong foundation for the students in the United States. It wasn't always enough of a defense, though, to help them navigate new systems or find the information they needed in a school where they did not feel comfortable, safe, or welcomed.[2] Although the students may have benefited from the social capital created when many adults took notice of them, the backing from their family or community wasn't always enough of a buffer at the larger high school. My relationship with the students could not always make a difference when the safety net had so many holes through which they could fall.

## Teacher–Student Expectations

This consideration changed markedly after I began the study, and I also had to help students understand what I could and could not do. For the most part, students knew that I was no longer *their* teacher and did not ask me for help with their papers or schoolwork. The very facts that they were in school as seniors, and that only a selected handful would graduate within the four-year expectation of schools around the nation, meant that they were strong individuals with an incredible work ethic, had overcome various barriers, and were, in short, people who knew how to survive and even thrive.

The interview relationship, whether with former students or strangers, is usually one in which differentials exist in position and power. It is important to realize this aspect when asking for permission to interview, giving participants the option to donate their time voluntarily, and providing permission to withdraw at any time. Although the researcher states these conditions and presents them as options, if the participants feel indebted to the interviewer, then withdrawal may not be a real choice in their minds.

### Researcher's Ability to Help

I had to understand my ability to give assistance, do what I could, and, more importantly, help students learn how to help themselves. Coming to these realizations marked a growth process in me as well; however, the students needed to understand my limitations and the difference in my role as a researcher rather than a teacher. It was the tightrope that I walked in doing this research. Because this is a study on the care ethic, the relationship that resulted between the interviewer and interviewees mimicked the relationship that develops between the teacher and the students. The more I interviewed the participants and got to know them, the more inclined I was to give help, if they asked.

### Research Design

In this study, many aspects of the educational process for adolescent immigrants deserved focus. I felt that many of them needed *fixing*, such as the way resources were allocated, the pull-out aspect of the program, the way language was taught, and the lack of support in the neighborhood home schools. This study has tried to focus on what *did* work; it is about how students, teachers, and an insightful principal created a positive learning environment at the Newcomer Academy. I can only hope that further work can be done in the neighborhood high schools to create an equally supportive environment there. The participants I interviewed were attendees at a school where they enjoyed the experience of learning.

## Narrative Inquiry

To document and analyze caring relationships in schools, I turned to oral narratives by gathering in-depth interviews from teachers, students, administrators, and support personnel. I used oral narratives to capture the first-hand accounts of experiences from teachers and students in an effort to understand what encourages these relationships and impedes them from forming. The use of in-depth interviews helped reconstruct an experience or reality (Grele, 1998) that encouraged interaction between me, as the researcher, and the subjects by creating the possibility of going beyond conventional stories (Gluck & Patai, 1991). Oral narratives further give voice to those who have sometimes been overlooked or remain voiceless in the research process. These narratives also give voice to participants, especially, when a new audience hears them (Perks & Thomson, 1998).

Moreover, narratives and the listening techniques involved in their collection are sometimes considered a feminist approach in that they involve the passage of stories from one generation to another (Gluck & Patai, 1991). Oral history traditions and feminist history thrive together and bring stories to light that have sometimes been hidden or represented in silences. In this way, collecting narratives can be an appropriate way to approach the practice or tradition of caring, which itself is often a seemingly hidden or invisible phenomenon. Oral narratives, then, in their use of evocative memories along with the reflective nature of memory and storytelling would be an appropriate methodology for capturing and giving voice to the care ethic in schools and schooling.

Portelli, a noted Italian oral historian, said that "Oral sources tell us not just what people did but what they wanted to do, what they believed they were doing, and what they now think they are doing" (1998, p. 67). Westerman (1998) felt that oral narratives were a way of giving testimony of an important experience, or a rising to consciousness. The best testimonies, he told us, are those that are easy to understand, get the point across, and reach people on an emotional, moral, and intellectual level. In addition, Frisch (1990) and Mace (1998) indicated that oral narratives, when put to paper, are co-created by the interviewee and the interviewer with a shared authority in preserving the oral narrative accounts in print form.

This narrative technique has often been used to capture a social history or events in which many participants are involved. This form of data collection is a way to unpack the layers of shared memories (Thompson, 2000), examine them, and attempt to document the deep connections that are formed and created in the process of a shared event such as schooling. The collection of stories from many sources allows the participants to voice their views about the events that they see taking shape before them. The permutations and nuances of a story collected in this way take advantage of the subtleties of memory (Thompson, 2000). The collection of stories recreates a kind of collective memory that goes beyond the actual facts (Bal, Crewe, & Spitzer, 1999). The depth of the stories allows subtle attitudes to emerge in these stories that surround the care or caring experience.

Portelli said that oral narratives create a sense of meaning beyond a reliable description of the event. Stories are not necessarily objective; rather, the interviewer actually becomes a part of the process of making sense of an experience (1991). However, oral sources are not always reliable or exact with regard to fact. This unreliability is not a weakness, but a strength: Errors, inventions, and myths lead us through and beyond facts to a meaning that points past the details (Portelli, 1991, p. 2). In addition, researchers have cautioned that a memory can sometimes be distorted, inaccurate, or "a treacherous thing" (Friedlander, 1998, p. 318). Hearing an event or description from a variety of sources creates a shared experience that resonates with the listener and pushes beyond any one informant's limitations or boundaries. This, it creates an experience that goes deeply toward a universal truth through imagination or symbolism (Portelli, 1991).

I chose to use oral narratives because the subtlety of the process is well suited to the subtle, yet powerful nature of the care experience.[3]

## *Use of Memory*

Memory is increasingly recognized as an important source of information (Bal, Crewe, & Spitzer, 1999). Schooling is certainly a shared experience with combined memories when teachers and students recollect them; however, the memory of a school goes beyond knowing with the mind. Memories are often collected as sensory data, and not only as mental knowing:

> When walking in a wet street, for example, one avoids stepping into a puddle not because of a conscious decision, but because "somehow" one knows that not avoiding the puddle results in wet feet (Bal, Crewe, & Spitzer, 1999, p. iv).

The memory evoked by a wet street today, perhaps, brings back a full experience that includes the mind, senses, and a kind of knowing that we call knowledge of life or life's lessons. When we remember our own positive experiences about schooling (or likewise, the negative experiences), the full experience comes back. These memories, which seem to become a present thought, can be sparked by a smell, word, gesture, conversation, food, event at a child's school, or some other combination of stimuli. Indeed, history can be called the voices of the past. When I interviewed the teachers and students in this study, I tried to make use of this fuller way of knowing that included sensory and emotional data, as well as actual facts, to make sense of the experience of care.

## Shared and Collective Memories

The memory of our schooling is collective and something that we share with our classmates, but the experience isn't the same for everyone. We can also have very private memories with a teacher or a special friend. It is in these more private memories that caring seems to take hold, and it is from memory that students and teachers can speak of their experience. Carl Glickman told of his visit to a highly accomplished, progressive school that has been existence for more than 20 years. A daughter and mother walked beside him after the meeting and tried to convey to him why the school was so important for both of them. They tried to say that it was more important than what happened in classrooms, based on their experiences at the school:

> "What we all told you in that meeting was what we do at this school, but that's not the most important part of our place" (Yael, the daughter says). (Yael's) mother adds, "It's hard to explain to others. When you attend this school, it never leaves you. It is with you forever... What you need to know is that we are standing on sacred ground." Yael nods quietly... (Glickman, 2003, p. 29)

In Ladson-Billings' study entitled *Dreamkeepers: Successful Teachers of African American Children*, the author was taken back to her own childhood memories of positive experiences with her teachers (2009). Her retelling made the research resonate in a kind of present universal way that transcended the time and place of the study. Memory can be incorporated into the study in just this way (Mace, 1998).

In a group retelling of an event or shared experience such as schooling, the informant or narrator will show points of intersection and divergence on a topic. A group interview will include several participants who inform an experience or event from multiple points of view or perspectives and create opportunities for reflection and retelling of the event (Mace, 1998). In the process of the group interaction and points of intersection with the interviewer or other interviewees, a shared experience emerges in which new details surface. New information, which could have been hidden or forgotten, and new ways of seeing a situation emerge. The multi-faceted aspect of a group's shared oral narrative gives a multi-faceted reflection of a situation and adds depth and richness to the experience (Mace, 1998).

Reflection or reflectivity can be an important part of research and the learning process, as described in the ethics of care. Reflexivity and reciprocity are key components in the care process: a time when the student feels confirmed or recognized (Noddings, 2003). Mace told us that in a group setting, the telling is as much about communicating as it is about creating (1998). One person echoes or retells another's description, and the telling of one story can cause another to reflect and share about the same or similar account. Delayed effects or reflections can occur after the fact with regard to the participants as well (Mace, 1998). Through the group process, a kind of eloquent consensus takes place. In guiding the discussions, the narrator is always a part of the process and becomes one of the characters in the unfolding of the experience (Portelli, 1991).

In summary, this study uses oral narratives to generate nuanced accounts of an individual's private experience of school and helps create the public reality in a full, rich manner that befits the experience itself. Oral narratives draw from a wealth of experiences to give a rich retelling of these shared memories. González, Moll, and Amanti (2005) quoted Willis in the beginning of one of their studies:

> The problem with many empirical data, empirically presented, is that they can be flat and uninteresting . . . In my view, well-grounded and illuminating analytic points flow only from bringing concepts into a relationship with the messiness of ordinary life, somehow recorded. (Willis, 2000, p. xi)

In their study of theorizing between households and schools, González, Moll, and Amanti involved teachers in authentic research that led "to innovations in both theory and practice" (2005, p. 23). These authors described an internal process that takes place within a researcher, who works both within the theoretical underpinnings of the university and the practical experiences of the field. Such working between theory and practice forms the basis of this research. The researcher moved from her practices and experiences in the school setting and informed these experiences with the richness of the care theory. Further, the oral narratives offer testimony (Westerman, 1998) that touches the reader in multiple layers. As such, it has a more lasting and far-reaching impact on the reader (Mace, 1998) and offers a natural way to capture the care experience.

## Researcher's Memory

If I think back to my own childhood, I have pleasant memories for the most part. I have chosen to remember these instances and let them outweigh other detracting memories. My first schooling was in France. The flood of memories I have from living as a child in Europe far outweighs the language barrier and resultant experiences in the French kindergarten class. Was it because at that age, the academic expectations were not so dramatic? Was it because I had such a strong base in my mature, older parents?

Later, when I returned to the United States, began to lose my eyesight, and had to wear thick glasses, were these inconveniences overshadowed by the amazing peer group, stimulating teachers and, again, invigorating family experiences? Perhaps the circumstances were a little like childbirth, in which the new child far outweighs any discomfort of the pregnancy and birth process. In this way, the narratives capture the predominant tenor and emotions of the students. If their internal fiber demonstrates the strength to survive, the students may suppress problems or not mention them because a show of weakness might set them back. In contrast, other students talk about their problems as something they lived through and realize that in telling them, they are stronger than any obstacle that might come in their way.

## Reader's Memory and Collective Notion of School

From our childhood, we may we have a memory of school—some notion of what school is or should be. Schools may not be able to continue or persist in the same ways as the institution that endures in our memory. Schools have to change because students and their needs have changed for many reasons. Schools and the way they look may need to change because the demands placed on students to prepare for our global economy are different; because students may have needs we did not have as students; because we are moving into an information age, dominated by the media; or simply because we now know of the importance of considering students' thoughts and feelings along with intellectual needs in the learning process.

Some parents have attended the same school that their children attend today. Even if the parents haven't attended that neighborhood home school, they feel that they are participants if their children attend, and that it is their school. Adults who live in the neighborhood and support the school with their tax dollars also feel that the school is their school, and that they can place expectations on the role of the school in generating productive future members of the community. This attitude contributes to the community feelings of ownership of the schools in their community: The students who attend these schools will eventually work in their businesses and become the citizens who vote and make decisions that directly impact the community after they graduate.

When the secretary of education spoke of closing under-performing schools, changing the school structure or governance patterns, and making other innovative changes, our first response might be emotional due to our sense of ownership or involvement with that school. Families in rural communities have struggled with a great sense of loss at closing community schools and consolidating with schools from other communities. The emotional investment that surrounds a school, especially our school, runs deep, and the significance of the school surpasses that of the actual school building itself.

Schooling and learning are universal experiences. Because we have all attended schools, readers will also have a response to the narrations. When we begin to remember a favorite teacher, similar notions surface; we remember that experience, even if we can't remember other details of the class, school, or subject matter.

Memories of a favorite teacher can evoke a plethora of emotions. When we felt cared for, our imagination was stirred by that person who had a vision for us. A bond was created that did not tie us down, but rather set us free to grow toward who we would become. Young people yearn for someone in their lives who can help them come in contact with whom they truly are.

## Narrative as a Universal Artifact

The narrative nature in which information is conveyed creates a rich and powerful context for telling the story or experience of schooling. The expressions encompass an intellectual, emotional, and sometimes visceral response in the listener and reader. Often, the student's voice, or even that of the teacher, is heard through the voices of others. In this study, we will hear their voices directly. Finally, in drawing from these narratives, universal truths with applicability and resonance in any school setting can be distilled and conveyed. The ways in which these teachers and students respond have implications beyond a school for new immigrants or, for that matter, beyond any school setting. The universal appeal of the stories affects us as readers in the same multi-dimensional way that any good story does.

In his fiction, Tobias Wolff (2004) spoke of how imagination can be used to transform a student from a working-class family consciousness and mindset into someone who can function in a different world.[4] The importance of care and the way students are treated and approached in a classroom, as well as the imaginative responses from students who can see themselves in the way the teacher suggests or imagines have import far beyond the relationships that form. They can be the very essence of a transformative journey that takes students to new levels of thought and a new standard in educational performance.

> *If you don't mind going places without a map, follow me.*
> —Ruth Behar, *The Vulnerable Observer* (1996, p. 33)

> *The journey from the head to the heart,*
> *The most important, least direct,*
> *A road with no map.*
> —Barbara McKinley, *Dear Muse* (1995, p. 35)

# APPENDIX B

## School Data

The following data gives some demographic information about the New-comer Academy, as compared to three of the neighborhood schools in the Samuelson school district from the years of the study.

| Category | Stafford High School | Kiowa High School | Newcomer Academy | Ashford High School |
|---|---|---|---|---|
| Number of Students | 1,599 | 1,520 | 190 | 2,101 |
| **Proficiencies Performance on Tests—Reading and Math** | | | | |
| Reading | 71.3% | 67.1% | 33.0% | 93.4% |
| Math | 46.9% | 40.4% | 63.0% | 84.7% |
| **Students by Sub Population** | | | | |
| ESL | 36.1% | 24.0% | 88.9% | 3.5% |
| ED | 77.1% | 77.9% | 90.0% | 18.5% |
| At-Risk | 83.9% | 83.8% | 91.1% | 36.4% |
| **Students Profiles** | | | | |
| Gender | | | | |
| Female | 50.3% | 50.2% | 51.6% | 48.3% |
| Male | 49.7% | 49.9% | 48.4% | 51.7% |

*(continued)*

*Care & Advocacy: Narratives from a School for Immigrant Youth*, pages 161–162
Copyright © 2012 by Information Age Publishing

| Category | Stafford High School | Kiowa High School | Newcomer Academy | Ashford High School |
|---|---|---|---|---|
| **Race/Ethnicity** | | | | |
| African-American | 13.4% | 12.6% | 3.2% | 7.5% |
| Asian | 2.2% | 0.6% | 7.4% | 5.9% |
| Hispanic | 77.2% | 81.4% | 88.9% | 23.0% |
| Native American | 0.2% | 0.1% | 0.0% | 0.3% |
| White | 6.9% | 5.3% | 0.5% | 63.3% |
| LEP exemption | 5.0% | 0.1% | 89.4% | 0.0% |
| Attendance Rates | 87.5% | 85.3% | 39.0% | 93.0% |
| Funding per Student | $412 | $461 | $1,636 | $300 |
| Completion Rate | 67.1% | 48.4% | Freshmen and Sophomore only | 89.5% |
| **Teacher Data** | | | | |
| Gender | | | | |
| Female | 62.9% | 59.9% | 67.7% | 62.9% |
| Male | 37.1% | 40.1% | 32.3% | 37.1% |
| Race/Ethnicity | | | | |
| African-American | 16.8% | 10.2% | 6.9% | 4.8% |
| Asian | 3.5% | 0.6% | 1.9% | 1.8% |
| Hispanic | 17.5% | 30.6% | 8.8% | 11.4% |
| Native American | 0.7% | 0.0% | 0.0% | 0.0% |
| White | 61.5% | 58.6% | 82.4% | 82.0% |

# Poems Written after the Death of Juan and My Mother

## For the students: Para los estudiantes

1.
Life is a blanket
we put on
*como cubierto*
that warms us.

*Como dices Alberto:*
*No te olvides de Mexico.*

Who can or will? *Quien puede?*

From these moments.
Moments such as these,
We come together.
And from these moments,
we move.

*Care & Advocacy: Narratives from a School for Immigrant Youth,* pages 163–166
Copyright © 2012 by Information Age Publishing

**163**

Must move.

It's how we
make our dreams.
*"Toda la vida es sueño,
y los sueños, sueños son."*

Remembering,
and more importantly,
*mas importante,*
living,
in this moment.

---

## Poems About the Pictures of My Mom in My Classroom—12/04/04

1.

It was as though she was *there*
looming over our class—with us.
moving through the mediums we avail ourselves
of. Chemicals. Photographic
paper. The precision lenses
of our modern cameras,
captured—*and released,*
She, and my father,
reside here with us
in our life here.
among our plants.
and flowers.

The care she's given me—
lives in us.

The way I teach. The way we learn.
*This caring business called school.*
Do you see this? How she is here with us?
How important is it for
us to know—
all of this matters?

This pencil.
This word.
This thought.
Our prayers. Our hopes.
The journey we move on, together.
The highway we have walked
to be here at this place.
At this time. Here and now.


2.

Who was giving the strength?
And who received it?
Who was supporting whom?

My mother, once, in the
forefront.
Yanet, who threw up, waiting so
politely for her teacher to give permission
to leave the room—Yanet, who threw up there
on the floor of the classroom,
rather than disobey. And Esbedey, who
fainted and
could not breathe
rather than be chastised
for doing something wrong.

These—the wise, maternal ones,
Mature and enduring, like *her*—
These students, they, expressed in their silent actions
as she did,
and still, I did not see her.

I was like the chatty, happy ones.
who love their *salon* because
they can be themselves,
absorbed in their own
world.

Can we ever move out of our
tiny orbs?

Can we blend, merge, move beyond?

*The Guide,* just there, in the picture,
here in fact, with us.

*What does it mean to say*
*we care?*


3.

You students, children here, many
without your mothers
or fathers,
do you see that she
is here with us?

Perhaps through me
or perhaps just here—
With us as we move
to our new
place,
saying, *it's all right.*

*It's all right.*

*Everything is all right.*

# A Roadmap of a Student's Life

This roadmap is a depiction of one adolescent immigrant student's life. Her story is somewhat representative of others who came to the United States as a teenager.

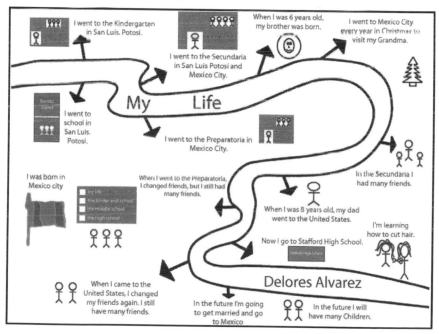

I went to the Kindergarten in San Luis. Potosi.

When I was 6 years old, my brother was born.

I went to Mexico City every year in Christmas to visit my Grandma.

I went to the Secundaria in San Luis Potosi and Mexico City.

My Life

I went to school in San Luis. Potosi.

I went to the Preparatoria in Mexico City.

I was born in Mexico city

my life
the kinder and school
the middle school
the high school

When I went to the Preparatoria, I changed friends, but I still had many friends.

In the Secundaria I had many friends.

When I was 8 years old, my dad went to the United States.

I'm learning how to cut hair.

Now I go to Stafford High School.

Delores Alvarez

When I came to the United States, I changed my friends again. I still have many friends.

In the future I'm going to get married and go to Mexico

In the future I will have many Children.

created by Jill Wolf

# *Photograph Described in Chapter 3*

This photograph is described in Chapter 3. Several pictures of my mom and students were somehow joined. In this photo we see my mother in her bed and two students from one of my classes. The window of the bedroom overlapped with the door to the classroom. The medicine shelf in her bedroom is next to the bookshelf from the classroom. The student next to her is Juan, who is discussed in Chapter 3.

# *Notes*

## Chapter 1

1. Teachers, administrators, staff members, and support personnel who have been interviewed are from the Academy, as this is the school where formative relationships were created. The students who recalled their experiences there were seniors at the time of their interviews. As such, they had been attending their neighborhood school for two years. The students had an opportunity to compare the two schools from this perspective. For the most part, their interviews took place in the libraries of the two neighborhood schools.

2. As a researcher, I followed a similar path. I taught the students for their first two years at the Newcomer Academy; then I took time off to finish my coursework at the university. When I returned to teach, the only position that was available for me was at Stafford High School, one of the neighborhood schools. While on campus one day, I saw a group of my former students in an advisory with a permanent substitute. I asked if I could become their advisory teacher and was able to stay with these students through their junior year. I graduated from the university the same year as the first graduating class from the Newcomer Academy.

3. These first-hand teaching experiences and observations at the Academy and Stafford High School, coupled with the observations over four years at Robert E. Lee, the neighborhood complex where the Academy was housed, gave me an opportunity to observe the similarities and differences among the three schools on a day-to-day basis. As a researcher, I also had the opportunity for multiple interviews and the review of many school documents, both public and private. As a participant observer, I took part in the various activities in these schools both while I was employed and afterward. These observations, participations, interviews, and document reviews took place from the fall 2004 to spring 2008.

# Chapter 8

1. Advocacy can take many forms, depending on the role of the person who advocates for a student. Broadly speaking, advocacy is putting the student's interests first. For further discussions of the importance of advocacy, see Anderson (2009), *Advocacy leadership: Toward a post-reform agenda in education*; Reyes, Scribner, & Scribner (1999), *Lessons from high-performing Hispanic schools: Creating learning communities*; and Shapiro & Stefkovich (2001), *Ethical leadership & decision making in education: Applying theoretical perspectives to complex dilemmas.*

2. The social and emotional aspects of learning are well documented on the collaborative for academic, social, and emotional learning (CASEL) website. CASEL is a non-profit organization based in Chicago, IL.

3. The personal aspect, in addition to social, emotional, and academic aspects of education is discussed on the KPM Approach to Children website. The Atma Vidya Educational Foundation developed this approach in Kerala, India.

# Chapter 10

1. Four of the participants in this team were key informants for this study and have remained with the Newcomer Academy for many years. They are named as authors in this document because of their contributions to the study. The other participants remain anonymous.

2. The teachers at the Newcomer Academy all had training from the district in SIOP, or Sheltered Instructional Observational Protocol; DL, or Differentiated Learning; as well as Q-TEL, Quality Teaching for English Learning.

   SIOP, or Sheltered Instruction Observation Protocol, is a methodology for teachers to provide a sheltered learning environment for English language learners in the classroom. It was originally designed for intermediate- to advanced-level language learners to transition into the classroom while still learning English. Lessons contain both content and language-learning goals. The instructor and curriculum support the lessons with vocabulary, visual organizers, or more detailed explanations for the textbook or lecture. The methodology was first outlined in Echivarrea, J., Short, D., Vogt, M. (2007), *Making Content Comprehensible for English Learners: The SIOP Model* (3rd ed.). New York, NY: Pearson Longman-Allyn Bacon.

   DL, or Differentiated Learning, has a focus on learning in the classroom by facilitating a focus on the diverse populations in the classroom. It helps teachers work with students by using different avenues toward learning. This method is often associated with integrating special education students into mainstream classrooms. An early proponent of this method has been Carol Ann Tomlinson. A recent publication is the following: Tomlinson, C., & McTighe, J. (2006). *Integrating Differentiated Instruction and Understanding by Design. Washington, DC: ASCD* Publication.

   Q-TEL, or Quality Teaching for English Learners, is a SIOP methodology developed and used by WEST Ed consulting. Some of its principles are included in the following: Walqui, A., & van Lier, L. (2010). *Scaffolding the*

*Academic Success of Adolescent English Language.* San Francisco, CA: West Ed Publications.

At the Newcomer Academy, the SIOP training was done once or twice, but the Q-TEL program involved training teachers in San Francisco for two weeks with numerous follow-ups onsite at the school. The teachers who were trained then become trainers who will train other staff members.

Rob's analogy in the conversation regarding SIOP may actually have meant that a number of the students were at a level lower than intermediate to advanced levels with their English usage, and that all of the teachers needed to learn to be adaptive beyond their training, regardless of what the methodology entailed. Perhaps because Q-TEL has onsite consultants, he referred to that methodology as going beyond the others.

3. Some programs are in place now that encourage vocational learning at the high school. The students take five years to complete the program, and the high school and local vocational institution work in conjunction with each other. The students graduate with job skills and can move to the next level in their transition to a new country with a vocational skill, which can sustain the students and their family while they continue on an educational track. See, for instance, The High School-to-College Transition Project (HS2C) created as a part of a network convened by the Center of Excellence in Leadership of Learning at the University of Indianapolis.

# Appendix A

1. The topics in this section are from a discussion by David A. Resnik on ethics in medical research, given at Wichita State University, fall 2009.
2. I have dealt with the importance of the social capital that is created between the adults in the Newcomer Academy and the students in Intergenerational Experiences that Create Social Capital in a School for Recent Hispanic/Latino Adolescent Immigrants. Stanton-Salazar (1979) wrote a seminal work on the importance of social capital with youth from marginalized populations.
3. In the article mentioned above, I discussed how oral narrative is well suited to capturing the caring exchanges that take place between adults and children, teachers and students, or other adults in a school setting and the youth who attend there. The voices of teachers or staff members (los abuelitos) are often unheard or interpreted by others, if heard at all. In this study, we hear their voices directly. Finally, in drawing from these full transcripts, the narratives distill and convey universal truths that have applicability and resonance in any school setting. We know from literary traditions that the story of one person or family can have universal power and appeal (Lee, 1988; Tolstoy, 2000; Twain, 1994). The oral narrative tradition allows for participants to tell their story in a simple and compelling way. Nuances and subtleties are allowed to arise because of the trust that develops between the researcher and participant due to the time they spend together.

The narratives hail from a transitional high school for immigrant students, but from the depth of the responses, we can see that they could also apply to other school settings. In this way, theory and practice inform one another, and the research from the field joins and creates new theory. The narratives hearken from an oral, literary heritage and blend well with the *care* theory and its focus on the relational aspects of teaching and learning. Oral narratives are often passed from one generation to another, so the use of this tradition with the depiction of the role of the grandparents also proves fruitful. The blending of these three traditions—oral narratives, care theory, and intergenerational investigation—creates a merging of method and message that allows a rich and full account of the participants' experiences.

4. The power of imagination is a largely overlooked aspect of the educational process or what we would call human development. We recognize the power of the imagination in literature but do not seem to understand that it is through the imagination that a student can grow into a new way of knowing. The imagination is sparked in the intergenerational relationships, especially those with older staff members. Grandchildren or youth speak of the magic and playfulness of these exchanges. Interestingly, this idea seems to be entering the literature in the area of computer usage in intergenerational exchanges. See, for instance, Vetere, F., Davis, H., Gibbs, M., & Howard, S. (2009). The Magic Box and Collage: Responding to the Challenge of Distributed Intergenerational Play.

# References

Anderson, G.L. (2009). *Advocacy leadership: Toward a post-reform agenda in education.* New York, NY: Routledge.

Argyris, C. (1999). Tacit knowledge and management. In R.J. Sternberg & J.A. Horvath (Eds), *Tacit knowledge in professional practice: Researcher and practitioner perspectives,* (pp. 123–140). Mahwah, NJ: Lawrence Erlbaum Associates, Inc.

Baker-Miller, J. (1976). *Toward a new psychology of women.* Boston: Beacon Press.

Bal, M., Crewe, J., & Spitzer, L. (1999). *Acts of memory: Cultural recall in the present.* Hanover, NH: University Press of New England.

Beck, L. (1994). *Reclaiming educational administration as a caring profession.* New York, NY: Teachers College Press.

Beck, L., & Murphy, J. (1994). *Ethics in educational programs: An expanding role* Thousand Oaks, CA: Corwin Press.

Behar, R. (1996). *The vulnerable observer: Anthropology that breaks your heart.* Boston, MA: Beacon Press.

Bellah, R., Madsen, R., Sullivan, W., Swidler, A., & Tipton, S. (1985). *Habits of the Heart.* Berkley, CA: University of California Press.

Bennett, J. (2008). Book review: Immigrant students and literacy: Reading, writing, and remembering, by Gerald Campano. New York: Teachers College Press, 2007. *Educational Administration Quarterly, 44*(2), 296.

Bennett, J., & Jaradat, M. (2011). Adolescent immigrant education: It's about more than learning English. *Journal of Cases in Educational Leadership,* 3–25. doi: 10.1177/15555458911404352.

Berry, B., & King, T. (2005). *Recruiting and retaining National Board Certified teachers for hart-to-staff, low-performing schools: Silver bullets or smart solutions.* Chapel Hill, NC: The Southeast Center for Teaching Quality.

Bhabha, H. (1994). *The location of culture.* New York, NY: Routledge.

---

*Care & Advocacy: Narratives from a School for Immigrant Youth,* pages 175–183
Copyright © 2012 by Information Age Publishing

Blanchard, K. (2010). *Leading at a higher level.* Retrieved from http://books. google.com/books

Blankstein, A., Houston, P., & Cole, R. (2008). *Sustaining professional learning communities.* Thousand Oaks, CA: Corwin Press.

Blasé, J., & Anderson, G. (1995). *The micropolitics of educational leadership: From control to empowerment.* New York, NY: Teachers College Press.

Bogotch, I. (2002). Educational leadership and social justice: Practice into theory. *Journal of School Leadership, 12*(2), 138–156.

Brown, K. M., & Wynn, S. R. (2007). Teacher retention issues: How some principals are supporting and keeping new teachers. *Journal of School Leadership, 17*(6), 664–698.

Buber, M. (1965). *Between man and man.* New York, NY: Macmillan.

Buber, M. (1966). *I and thou.* W. Kaufmann (Trans.). New York, NY: Charles Scribner's & Sons. (Original work published 1970)

Campano, G. (2007). *Immigrant students and literacy: Reading, writing, and remembering.* New York: Teachers College Press.

Campbell, D. E. (2004). *Democracy: A practical guide to multicultural education* (3rd ed.). Upper Saddle River, NJ: Pearson Merrill-Prentice Hall.

Carnegie, D. (1982). *How to win friends and influence people* (Revised ed.). New York, NY: Simon Schuster. Original work published 1936.

Chamot, A., & O'Malley, J. (1994). *CALLA handbook: Implementing the cognitive academic language learning approach.* White Plains, NY: Addison Wesley Publishing.

Cibulka, J. (2009). *Meeting urgent national needs in P–12 education: Improving relevance, evidence, and performance in teacher preparation.* Washington D.C.: National Council for Accreditation of Teacher Education.

Cochran-Smith, M. (1995). Uncertain allies: Understanding the boundaries of race and teaching. *Harvard Educational Review, 65*(4), 541–571.

Council of Chief State School Officers (CCSSO). (1996). Interstate school leaders licensure consortium: Standards for school leaders (ILLCS). Washington, D.C.: Author.

Crowther, F., Ferguson, M., & Hann, L. (2008). *Developing teacher leaders: How teacher leadership enhances school success.* Thousand Oaks, CA: Corwin Press.

Cushman, K. (2005). *Fires in the bathrooms: Advice for teachers from high school students.* New York, NY: The New Press.

Darling-Hammond, L. (2000). *Solving the dilemmas of teacher supply, demand, and quality.* New York: National Commission on Teaching and America's Future.

Darling-Hammond, L. (2003). Keeping good teachers: Why it matters, what leaders can do. *Educational Leadership, 60*(8), 6–13.

Darling-Hammond, L. (2004). Inequality and the right to learn: Access to qualified teachers in Califorina's public schools. *Teachers College Record, 106*(10), 1936–1966.

Darling-Hammond, L., LaPointe, M., Meyerson, D., Orr, M.T., & Cohen, C. (2007). *Preparing school leaders for a changing world: Lessons from exemplary leadership development programs.* Stanford, CA: Stanford University, Stanford Educational Leadership Institute.

Doehring, C. (1995). *Taking care: Monitoring power dynamics and relational boundaries in pastoral care and counseling.* Nashville, TN: Abingdon Press.

Donaldson, G. A. (2001). *Cultivating leadership in schools: Connecting people, purpose, and practice.* New York, NY: Teacher's College Press.

Echevarria, J., Short, D., & Vogt, M. (2007). *Implementing the SIOP Model through effective professional development and coaching.* New York, NY: Allyn & Bacon Pearson Longman.

Feiman-Nemser, S. (2003). What new teachers need to learn. *Educational Leadership, 60*(8), 25–29.

Forster, E. M. (1988). *A room with a view.* New York, NY: Bantom Classic Random House.

Foster, M., Lewis, J., & Onafowora, L. (2005). Grooming great urban teachers. *Educational Leadership, 62*(6), 28–32.

Frisch, M. (1990). *A shared authority: Essays on the craft and meaning of oral and public history.* Albany, NY: State University of New York Press.

Furman, G., & Gruenewald, D. (2004). Expanding the landscape of social justice: A critical ecological analysis. *Educational Administration Quarterly, 40*(1), 47–76.

Gibbons, J., & Cummins, P. (2002). *Scaffolding language, scaffolding learning: Teaching second language learners in the mainstream classrooms.* New York, NY: Heinemann.

Gilligan, C. (1982). *In a different voice: Psychological theory & women's development.* Boston, MA: Harvard University Press.

Glickman, C. (2003). *Holding sacred ground: Essays on leadership, courage, and endurance in our schools.* New York, NY: Jossey-Bass.

Gluck, S., & Patai, D. (1991). *Women's words: The feminist practice of oral history.* New York, NY: Routledge.

Goldman, G. (2006). *Social intelligence: The new science of human relationships.* New York, NY: Bantam Random House.

Goldstein, L. (1997). *Teaching with love: A feminist approach to early childhood education (Rethinking Childhood, Vol. 1).* New York, NY: Peter Lang Publishing.

Goldstein, L. (2002). *Reclaiming caring in teaching and teacher education.* New York, NY: Peter Lang Publishing.

González, N., Moll, L., & Amanti, C. (2005). *Funds of knowledge: Theorizing practices in households, communities, and classrooms.* New York, NY: Routledge.

Gordon, S., Benner, P., & Noddings, N. (1996). *Caregiving: Readings in knowledge, practice, ethics, and politics.* Philadelphia, PA: University of Pennsylvania Press.

Grant, C., & Sleeter, C. (2007). *Doing multicultural education for achievement and equity.* New York, NY: Routledge.

Grele, R. (1998). Movement without aim: Methodological and theoretical problems in oral history. In R. Parks & A. Thomson (Eds.), *The oral history reader*, 393–401. New York, NY: Routledge.

Hamilton, D. (2009). *It's the thought that counts: Why mind over matter really works.* London: Hay House.

Hanushek, E., Kain, J., & Rivkin, S. (1998). *Teachers, schools, and academic achievement.* Hoover Institute, Stanford University: Working Paper National Bureau of Economic Research.

Hanushek, E., Kain, J., & Rivkin, S. (1999*). Do higher salaries buy better teachers?* Hoover Institute, Stanford University: Working Paper National Bureau of Economic Research.

Hanushek, E., Kain, J., & Rivkin, S. (2004). Why schools lose teachers. *Journal of Human Resources, 39*(2), 326–354.

Hargreaves, A. (2008a). Foreword to the second edition. In F. Crowther, M. Ferguson & L. Hann (Eds.), *Developing teacher leaders* (2nd ed.). Thousand Oaks, CA: Sage Publisher.

Hargreaves, A. (2008b). Leading professional learning communities: Moral choices & murky realities. In A. M. Blankstein, P. D. Houston & R. W. Coles (Eds.), *Sustaining professional learning communities.* Thousand Oaks, CA: Corwin Press.

Hess, F. M. (2003). *A license to lead? A new leadership agenda for America's schools.* Washington, DC: Progressive Policy Institute.

Hofstede, G., Hofstede, G., & Minkov, M. (2010). *Cultures and organizations: Software of the mind: Intercultural cooperation and its importance for survival* (3rd ed.). New York: McGraw-Hill.

Hord, S. (2004). *Learning together, leading together: Changing schools through professional learning communities.* New York, NY: Teachers College Press.

Ingersoll, R. (1998). The problem of out-of-field teaching. *Phi Delta Kappan, 79*(10).

Ingersoll, R. (2001a). Teacher turnover and teacher shortages: An organizational analysis. *American Educational Research Journal, 38*(3), 499.

Ingersoll, R. (2001b). The realities of out-of-field teaching. *Educational Leadership, 58*(8), 42–45.

Ingersoll, R. (2002). The teacher shortage: A case of wrong diagnosis and wrong prescription. *NASSP bulletin, 86*(631), 16–31.

Ingersoll, R. (2003). *Who controls teachers' work? Power and accountability in America's schools.* Boston, MA: Harvard University Press.

Jung, C. (1962). *Memories, dreams, and reflections.* A Jaffee (Ed.). (R. Winston & C. Winston, Trans.) London: Knopf Doubleday.

Katzenbach, J., & Smith, D. (2003). *The wisdom of teams: Creating the high-performance organization.* New York NY: Harper Paperbacks.

Kelly, S. (2004). An even history analysis of teacher attrition: Salary, teaching tracking, and socially disadvantaged schools. *The Journal of Experimental Education, 72*(3), 195–220.

Knight, J. (2007). *Instructional coaching: A partnership approach to improving instruction.* Thousand Oaks, CA: Corwin Press.

Koellner, L. (2002, July 30). *The importance of people.* Presentation to Boeing global enterprise employee involvement team. Seattle, WA. Retrieved October 8, 2011 from http://www.boeing.com/news/speeches/2002/koellner_020730.html

Krashen, S. (2010). *Explorations in language acquisition and use.* New York, NY: Heinemann.

Ladson-Billings, G. (2009). *The dreamkeepers: Successful teachers of African American children* (2nd ed.). San Francisco, CA: Jossey-Bass Inc Publishers.

Lampert, M. (2010). Learning teaching in, from, and for practice: What do we mean? *Journal of teacher education, 61*(1–2), 21–34.

Lawrence-Lightfoot, S. (1983). *The good high school: Portraits of character and culture.* New York, NY: Basic Books.

Lee, J., & Bean, F. (2004). America's changing color lines: Immigration, race/ethnicity, and multiracial identification. *Annual Review of Sociology, 30,* 221–242.

Leithwood, K., & Mascall, B. (2008). Collective leadership effects on student achievement. *Educational Administration Quarterly, 44*(4), 529–561.

Louis, K. S. (2003). School leaders facing real change: Shifting geography, uncertain paths. *Cambridge Journal of Education, 33*(3), 371–382.

Louis, K.S., Marks, H.M., & Kruse, S (1996). Teachers' professional community in restructuring schools. *American Educational Research Journal, 33*(4), 757–798.

Macc, J. (1998). Reminiscence as literacy: Intersection and creative moments. In R. Parks & A. Thomson (Eds.), *The oral history reader.* New York, NY: Routledge.

Macmurray, J. (1990). *Persons in Relation.* New York: Harper & Brother.

Marshall, C. (1992). School Administrators. *Educational Administration Quarterly, 28*(3), 368–386.

Marshall, C., & Anderson, G. (1995). Rethinking the public and private spheres: Feminist and cultural studies perspectives on the politics of education. In J. D. Scribner, & D. H. Layton (Eds.), *The study of educational politics: The 1994 commemorative yearbook of the Politics of Education Association 1969–1994.* Washington, DC: Falmer Press.

Marshall, C., & Gerstl-Pepin, C. (2005). *Re-framing educational politics for social justice.* New York, NY: Allyn and Bacon.

Maslow, A. (1970). *Motivation and personality* (3rd ed.). New York, NY: Harper & Row.

Mayeroff, M. (1971). *On caring.* New York, NY: HarperCollins Publishers.

McKinley, B. (1995). *Dear muse.* Austin, TX: Ingleside Press.

McKinley, B. (2001). *Song of the suburbs.* Austin, TX: Ingleside Press.

McKinley, B. (2006). *Second verse.* Austin, TX: Ingleside Press.

Meyer, J., & Rowan, B. (1991). Institutionalized organizations: Formal structure as myth and ceremony. In W. W. Powell & P. DiMaggio (Eds.), *The new institutionalism in organizational analysis.* Chicago, IL: University of Chicago Press.

Miller, R., & Rowan, B. (2006). Effects of organic management on student achievement. *American Educational Research Journal, 43*(2), 219.

Mink, B., & Lang, k. d. (1991). Constant craving. Recorded by k.d. lang. On Ingénue, Vancouver. British Columbia, CA: Sire Records.

Murphy, J. (2000). Governing America's schools: The shifting playing field. *The Teachers College Record, 102*(1), 57–84.

Murphy, J. (2005). Unpacking the foundations of ISLLC standards and addressing concerns in the academic community. *Educational Administration Quarterly, 41*(1), 154–191.

Murphy, J., Beck, L. G., Crawford, M., & Hodges, A. (2001). *The productive high school: Creating personalized academic communities.* Thousand Oaks, CA: Corwin Press.

Nieto, S. (1999). *The light in their eyes.* New York, NY: Teachers College Press.

Nieto, S. (2003). *What keeps teachers going?* New York, NY: Teachers College Press.

Noblit, G. (1993). Power and caring. *American Educational Research Journal, 30*(1), 23–28.

Noddings, N. (1984). *Caring: a feminine approach to ethics and moral education.* Berkeley, CA: University of California Press.

Noddings, N. (1995). *Philosophy of education.* Boulder, CO: Westview Press.

Noddings, N. (1996). The cared-for. *Caregiving: Readings in knowledge, practice, ethics, and politics,* 21–39.

Noddings, N. (2002). *Educating moral people: A caring alternative to character education.* New York, NY: Teachers College Press.

Noddings, N. (2003). *Caring: A feminine approach to ethics & moral education.* Berkeley, CA: University of California Press.

Noddings, N. (2005). *The challenge to care in schools: An alternative approach to education* (2nd ed.). New York, NY: Teacher's College Press.

Ogbu, J. (Ed.)(2008). *Minority status, oppositional culture, and schooling.* New York, NY: Routledge.

Olsen, L. (2008). *Made in America: Immigrant students in our public schools. 10th anniversary edition.* New York, NY: The New Press.

Orfield, G. (2004). *Losing our future: How minority youth are being left behind by the graduation rate crisis.* Boston, MA: Harvard University Press.

Perks, R., & Thomson, A. (1998). Critical developments: Introductions. In R. Parks & A. Thomson (Eds.), *The oral history reader.* New York, NY: Routledge.

Plato, C. (1995). *Phaedrus.* Nehamas, A. & Woodruff, P. (Trans.). Indianapolis, IN: Hackett Publishing Co., Inc.

Polite, V., & Davis, J. (1999). *African American males in school and society: Practices and policies for effective education.* New York, NY: Teachers College Press.

Portelli, A. (1991). *The death of Luigi Trastulli and other stories: Form and meaning.* Albany, NY: SUNY Press.

Portelli, A. (1998). What makes oral history different? In R. Parks & A. Thomson (Eds.), *The oral history reader.* New York, NY: Routledge.

Powell, A. G., Farrar, E., & Cohen, D. K. (1985). *The shopping mall high school: Winners and losers in the educational marketplace.* Boston, MA: Houghton-Mifflin.

Powell, W., & DiMaggio, P. (Eds.) (1991). *New institutionalism and organizational analysis.* Chicago, IL: University of Chicago Press.

Reyes, P., Scribner, J. D., & Scribner, A. P. (1999). *Lessons from high-performing Hispanic schools: Creating learning communities.* New York: NY: Teachers College Press.

Riis, P. (2003). Thirty years of bioethics: the Helsinki Declaration 1964–2003. *New Review of Bioethics, 1*(1), 15–25.

Rimmington, G., & Alagic, M. (2009). *Third place learning: Reflective inquiry into intercultural and global cage painting: Teaching-learning indigenous, intercultural worldviews.* Charlotte, NC: Information Age Publishing.

Romo, H., & Falbo, T. (1996). *Latino high school graduation: Defying the odds.* Austin, TX: University of Texas Press.

Rusch, E. A., & Marshall, C. (1995). *Gender filters at work in the administrative culture.* Paper presented at the annual meeting of the American Educational Research Association, San Francisco, CA.

Rutherford, J. (1990). *Identity: Community, culture, difference.* London: Lawrence and Wishart.

Salinger, J. D. (1991). *The catcher in the rye.* New York, NY: Little Brown Books.

Scarcella, R. (2003a). *Accelerating academic English: A focus on English language learners.* Oakland, CA: Regents of the University of California.

Scarcella, R. (2003b). *Academic English: A conceptual framework (Technical Report 2003-1).* Santa Barbara, CA: Linguistic Minority Research.

Scott, W. R. (2001). *Institutions and organizations.* San Francisco, CA: Jossey-Bass.

Sedlack, M. W., Wheeler, C. E., Pullin, D. C., & Cusick, P. A. (1986). *Selling students short: Classroom bargains and academic reform in the American high school.* New York, NY: Teachers College Press.

Senge, P. M., Cambron-McCabe, N., Lucas, T., Smith, B., Dutton, J., & Kleiner, A. (2000). *Schools that learn: A fifth discipline fieldbook for educators, parents, and everyone who cares about education.* New York, NY: Crown Random House.

Sergiovanni, T. (2007). *Rethinking leadership: A collection of articles.* San Francisco, CA: Corwin Press.

Sergiovanni, T., & Starratt, R. J. (2002). *Supervision: A redefinition.* Boston, MA: McGraw-Hill.

Sernak, K. (1998). *School leadership—Balancing power with caring.* New York, NY: Teachers College Press.

Shakespeare, W. (2004). As you like it. In E. Bevington, (Ed.). *The complete works of Shakespeare* (5th ed.). New York: W.W. Norton & Company, Inc.

Shakespeare, W. (2004). The Tempest. In E. Bevington, (Ed.). *The complete works of Shakespeare* (5th ed.). New York: W.W. Norton & Company, Inc.

Shamoo, A., & Resnik, D. (2009). *Responsible conduct of research.* Oxford, UK: Oxford University Press.

Shapiro, J. P. & Stefkovich, J. A. (2001). *Ethical leadership & decision making in education: Applying theoretical perspectives to complex dilemmas.* Mahwah, NJ: Lawrence Erlbaum Associates, Publishers.

Spillane, P. (2006). *Distributed leadership.* San Francisco, CA: Wiley, & Sons.

Spillane, J., & Diamond, J. (2007a). *Distributed leadership in practice.* New York, NY: Teachers College Press.

Stanton-Salazar, R. (1997). A social capital framework for understanding the socialization of racial minority children and youths. *Harvard Educational Review, 67*(1), 1–41.

Stockard, J., & Lehman, M.B. (2004). Influences on the satisfaction and retention of 1st-year teachers: The importance of effective school management. *Educational Administration Quarterly, 40*(5), 742–771.

Swanson, C.B. (2008). Cities in crisis: A special analytic report on high school graduation. Bethseda, MD: Editorial Projects in Education.

Tarlow, B. (1996). Caring: A negotiated process that varies. *Caregiving: Readings in knowledge, practice, ethics, and politics,* 56–82.

Texas Education Agency. (2001). Secondary school completion and dropouts in Texas public schools: 1999–00. Austin, TX: Author.

Texas Education Agency. (2009). School data retrieved from http://www.tea. state.ts.us.

Theoharis, G. (2009). *The school leaders our children deserve: Seven keys to equity, social justice, and school reform.* New York, NY: Teacher College Press.

Thompson, P. R. (2000). *The voice of the past: Oral history* (3rd ed.). Oxford: Oxford University Press.

Tolstoy, L. (2000). *Anna Karenina: A novel in eight parts.* R. Peavear & L. Volokhonsky (Trans.). New York, NY: Penguin Books. Original work published 1887.

Tomlinson, C., & McTighe, J. (2006). *Integrating differentiated instruction and understanding by design.* Washington, DC: ASCD Publication.

United Nations. (1975). *Helsinki Declaration.* Paper presented at the Conference on Security and Co-Operation in Europe. Helsinki, Finland: Author.

Valencia, R. R. (1997). Conceptualizing the notion of deficit thinking. In R. R. Valencia (Ed.), *The evolution of deficit thinking: Educational thought and practice.* Washington, DC: Falmer Press.

Valenzuela, A. (1999). *Subtractive schooling: US-Mexican youth and the politics of caring.* Albany, NY: State University of New York Press.

Valenzuela, A., Fuller, E., & Vasquez-Heilig, J. (2006). The disappearance of high school English language learners from Texas high schools. *Williams Review, 1,* 170–200.

Van Reken, R. E., & Pollock, D. C. (2009). *Third culture kids: Prototypes for understanding other cross-cultural kids* (2nd ed.). Boston, MA: Nicholas Brealey Publishing.

Vasquez-Heilig, J. (2011). Understanding the interaction between high-stakes graduation tests and English learners. *Teachers College Record, 113*(12), 1–25.

Veblen, T. (2008). *The theory of the leisure class.* Charleston, SC: Forgotten Books.

Vetere, F., Davis, H., Gibbs, M., & Howard, S. (2009). The magic box and collage: Responding to the challenge of distributed intergenerational play. *International Journal of Human-Computer Studies 67*(2), 165–178.

Walqui, A., & Van Lier, L. (2010). *Scaffolding the academic success of adolescent English language learners: A pedagogy of promise.* San Francisco, CA: West Ed.

Westerman, W. (1998). Central American refugee testimonies and performing life histories in the sanctuary movement. In R. Parks & A. Thomson (Eds.), *The oral history reader* (pp. 224–234). New York, NY: Routledge.

Williams, W. C. (1985). So much depends. In C. Tomlinson (Ed.), *William Carlos Williams: Selected poems.* New York, NY: New Directions Publishing.

Willis, P. (2000). *The ethnographic imagination.* Cambridge, UK: Polity Press.

Wilson, S., Floden, R., & Ferrini-Mundy, J. (2001). *Teacher preparation research: Current knowledge, gaps, and recommendations.* Seattle, WA: University of Washington, Center for the Study of Teaching and Policy.

Wright, S. H., Houston, S., Ellis, M., Holloway, S., & Hudson, M. (2003). Crossing racial lines: geographies of mixed-race partnering and multi-raciality in the United States. *Progress in Human Geography, 27*(4), 457–474.

Wolff, T. (2004). *Old School.* New York, NY: Vintange Books.

Yeats, W. B. (1970). Among school children. In D. G. Sanders, J. H. Nelson & M. L. Rosenthal (Eds.), *Chief modern poets of Britain and America: Poets of Britain* (Vol. 1). London, England: The Macmillan Company.